Universal Law

UNIVERSAL LAW

CREATING A NEW WORLD IN THE IMAGE OF ATLANTIS

COURTNEY BECK

Copyright © 2020 by Courtney Beck
All rights reserved. This book or any portion thereof may not be reproduced or used in any manner whatsoever without the express written permission of the author except for the use of brief quotations in a book review.

Courtney Beck
www.courtneybeck.co
courtney@courtneybeck.co

*To those dreaming of a new world, while still stuck
in the old one.*

Contents

Author's Note xiii
Acknowledgements xv
Also by Courtney Beck xvii

1. Universal Law 1
2. Your Choice 3
3. Law 1: Balance 6
4. The Sea 9
5. Learn from Atlantis 12
6. The Dream 15
7. Equality 17
8. Peace 20
9. Heracles 23
10. Caretakers 26
11. Kelipah 28
12. Gifts 32
13. Law 2: Gravity 35
14. Three Rules 38
15. Law 3: Transference 41
16. The Wave 44
17. Law 4: Elemental Law 46

18. Extinction 52
19. Damiascas 55
20. Law 5: Courage 57
21. A Peaceful Place 59
22. Origins of Kelipah 61
23. Law 6: Circumstance 63
24. Being Courageous 66
25. Lost 69
26. Law 7: Respect 71
27. A Safe Place to Hide 73
28. War 76
29. Law 8: Greed 80
30. Crops 82
31. Law 9: The Web of Life 84
32. Knowing 87
33. Excess 89
34. Law 10: Illusions 91
35. Currency 94
36. Information 97
37. Loving Spirits 100
38. Ignorance 104
39. Ancient People 107
40. Secrets 111
41. Slow 113
42. Super Waves 115

43. Fight 118
44. More 121
45. Law 11: Profit 123
46. Preparation 126
47. Adapt 129
48. Thoughtfulness 132
49. Shiva 135
50. Scholars 137
51. Emerald 140
52. Krishna's Perspective 142
53. Law 12: Regeneration 145
54. Law 13: Survival 149
55. Cities 153
56. Water 156
57. Restoration 158
58. Fire 161
59. Crystals 163
60. Builders 165
61. Law 14: Grace 167
62. Wounded 169
63. Vision 171
64. Law 15: Growth 173
65. Time 176
66. Help 179
67. Ripples 182

68. Righting Wrongs 184

69. Expectations 187

70. Changemakers 190

71. Purity 193

72. Commitment 195

73. 2020 200

74. Law 16: Convalescence 203

75. Kelipah: A Test 207

76. An Invitation 209

AUTHOR'S NOTE

Universal Law is the book I was too scared to publish.

There are the loving and beautiful words I channel that could fill a Hallmark card, and there is this book.

This book is the one I hid away on my laptop for years, hoping what I'd channeled would never come true, but it is, and now I wished I'd published it sooner.

The words you'll read are a direct transcript of what I received from a spirit guide, Krishna, who lived in Atlantis at the time of its fall. It is confronting at times, but also immensely beautiful and sets a standard of what we can achieve IF we understand what is possible and how to abide by Universal Law.

Thank you for reading.

Courtney

ACKNOWLEDGEMENTS

Completing this labor of love would not be possible, was it not for those who put up with my laboring.

To my incredible wife Jules London, the supernatural love, strength, and belief you offer me make this spiritual life possible. When so much of my life is in flux, you are my constant. Thank you for loving me when I'm light as a feather, fierce as a tornado, and everything else in between. I am so lucky to have you.

To my daughter, Isabella Mills, thank you for being our proof-reader. You're the only human I know fearless enough to ask a deity if he can make an apocalyptic warning friendlier.

To my friends and family who love me unconditionally, never batting an eyelid when I say I've spent the day battling demons or disappear for months at a time, I love you, and thank you.

And finally, to you, who supports my work, thank you for being a part of my story. Without you, I wouldn't be able to fulfill my purpose. It is you who this book is for, and it is our work together that will bring in a new age of Atlantis.

ALSO BY COURTNEY BECK

Conversations with Krishna

Awakened Souls

Akira

The Goddess Isis: Creation from Chaos

www.courtneybeck.co

UNIVERSAL LAW

Universal Laws are the rules and the ways of old, ways that were defined millions of years ago to keep the earth and its people in balance.

They are laws we cannot see, yet our understanding of them is imperative.

If earth is the school we are born to attend, the universe is the headmistress's office. It is where the decisions are made, and it is these unseen decisions that hold consequences for our past, present, and future.

We often question why events in our lives occur in the way they do, and this is universal law.

Universal law is the reason earth and the universe are rebalanced under specific timeframes, and it is the same reason so many species die out by our hands.

Universal law is what keeps the universe and all who exist

within it in balance, but this is not something humanity understands as we have lost touch with these principles.

What I will share with you in this book are the unseen laws that govern our universe and what you can do to work with them.

Much like Nostradamus made predictions of our earth, predictions will be made in this book. This is not so you can test if they come true, but so you have an opportunity to change.

We cannot alter your past, but we can help you transform your future if you listen and take heed of our warnings.

Take my words seriously, just as you would if you were standing inside the headmistress's office.

The playground you run in is a long way from the office, so if you wish to learn how to exist effortlessly in this world, it would be wise for you to know her rules. For the child in the playground who knows what occurs behind closed doors is not just wise; he or she runs the school as they have the foresight to know what is coming.

This book will give you the foresight to better run your own life and contribute to what the earth needs while you are doing it.

2

YOUR CHOICE

To run naked in a field, unaware of predators, will shorten your life by a significant amount.

To run naked in a field knowing what awaits you if you are not respectful of your environment, or how to work with each predatory element within it, will help you live a long and fruitful destiny.

Those who are wise are often underestimated because the skin they run in does not show the wisdom that lies within.

If you are wise, you will learn all you can about universal law as these laws are the predators in your life that appear unforeseen and with a bite stronger than anything physical in the earthly realm.

They are the predator that lies in the tree, just above you, out of sight, and the snake that lies in the grass as you run, unable to take your surroundings in fast enough.

If you are smart, knowing universal law will help you run with shoes on and avoid areas that may be unsafe.

The universal laws are not hard to learn, but most will never give them the time they need or deserve because they operate in a realm far above us. They go far and beyond the karmic records you hold, the good deeds you have done, or not done, and the lives you have led to reach this place. They are everything that does not make sense about our world, and why neglecting these laws have led us to the place on earth we are now.

If you are smart, you will learn what is unseen, as knowing what is unseen will reveal all on earth. Once you know the laws you are moving within, the laws' actions will reveal themselves on earth.

Just as running in the field with expert knowledge of it shows you where all of the animals are, you will see everything before others do.

What you must decide is whether you wish to live your life by them or not, whether you choose to believe in them or not and whether you will abide by them as a human in a world and universe you do not understand.

What you learn now will ultimately change your destiny and your life if you let these laws change you and be written into your karmic scripture.

Universal laws are a choice for human beings. You may

choose to follow them or not, but the consequences will be brought down upon you anyway.

Would you prefer to run naked and unaware or be a respectful runner and know how to avoid an uncertain and potentially dangerous destiny?

We do not promise the elixir of life, nor can we extend the life you are leading now, but we can empower you to run untamed with the heart of a lion and the tenacity of a snake. The laws will throw themselves at you anyway; you may as well catch them.

LAW 1: BALANCE

In the beginning, we were acutely aware of the laws that governed us because they were taught to us.

In the age of Atlantis, we knew the impact and power of universal law and worked with each law to elevate our creativity, impact, and ethics.

However, when Atlantis fell, and the new era took over, we saw a change and arrogance that swept the world. Human beings were in power and not in equality, and the universe and its laws fell into the distance.

Where the laws were once a large and influential part of our lives, they were now a whisper as human beings forgot their relationship with the universe and forged ahead on their own.

The life we have led on earth has not always been pretty, but it has been in balance. Atlantis was a time when this balance was seen in all its utter beauty and brilliance. Like a diamond shining brightly, Atlantis was a product that the earth created.

The earth bore Atlantis, and the earth destroyed it again when human beings decided they no longer needed the universe. The consequences of this decision are still seen today.

We will speak of Atlantis in this book as it is an original reference of what was and what could be again. It is the way forward and the light we could bring back to earth if human beings could release their petty ways and need for control.

Atlantis was a great and wondrous time in our history and something we wish for you to experience again.

In Atlantis, there was equality, and no-one went without. In Atlantis, love was in abundance. There were no abandoned children as abandonment did not exist. There was no crime because nothing was in lack.

The Atlanteans did not foresee the fall of their society before it came. It was a universal rebalance that caused this great city's downfall.

Balance does not allow for excess, and this is the first universal law.

A life lived in balance means there is enough for all and not just for one. When Atlantis tipped out of balance, those in power took even more from those who already went without.

In Atlantis, we saw the beauty of our history and the celebration of our creation fall within a single day, month, and year.

We will take you through the events of this time, so you may see the fall of Atlantis, why it happened, and what you must do to create your own Atlantis here on earth again. But first, you must learn the laws that created Atlantis are the same ones that made it fall.

To know universal law is to see the patterns that occur in our universe and for them not to be nameless and unknown. Universal law makes what is unknown known and allows us to make sense of what each pattern means.

Atlantis did not need to fall. There were signs.

In this book, I will take you through these signs, and you will learn why Atlantis fell, and in turn, you will learn how to make it rise again.

Equality and free power are possible on earth. Freedom with love and not hate is also possible. Life presents us with many opportunities to change. Will you take this one?

# THE SEA

The day the waves came was like any other day.

The people of Atlantis carried out their daily activities just as they had for many days and years before. They were not aware of what was coming, nor were they prepared for it.

When the first wave hit and took out their power systems, there was no light only sound. Just as in the beginning of the universe, there was no light and only sound.

What Atlantis did not expect to see was its downfall. And as their society fell out of balance, there were signs a wave was coming.

Abuse and power grew within specific individuals and groups in the city. Some spoke of technology and the ability of it to harness our destiny and others believed power should be equal, free, and available to us all. When there is equality, there is no power, only balance.

On the day Atlantis fell, the great goddess Thera wept in sorrow as the walls came down.

The waves consumed the city with a ferocity that was unseen or unheard of. Formerly the waves were Atlantis's friend.

As a city built on water, the city was powered and supported by the ocean. All of the elements (fire, air, earth & water) played a part in helping Atlantis thrive, and water had been no different.

Yet on this day, the sea erupted without warning, sending giant and encompassing waves through Atlantis. King Neptune's spear was thrown at a city that had once been the pride of the ocean.

It was as if penance was being paid for an unknown crime. However, the crime was known, and the people of Atlantis did nothing to stop it. Instead, they waited to see if the island would naturally restore its sense of balance.

The mistake Atlantis made was letting the darkness in.

The sea was always coming for Atlantis, but they had not prepared for it. Like a bushfire regenerates the earth, the sea washed Atlantis clean of the mistakes it had made. What the Atlanteans did not expect was that the sea would take everything.

If you are wise, you will hear the story of Atlantis, and recognize it as your own.

The sea is coming for us, and we must prepare for it. There will be a rebalance as inequality on earth in this time is so blinding and deafening to the universe; it cannot stand it any longer.

When the rebalance occurs, an opportunity to rebuild will be offered. When this time comes, will you respect the universal laws that govern you, or will you ignore them?

Will you feed those who are hungry, allowing the earth to stay in balance, or will you build an Atlantis more like ancient Rome?

These choices are yours to make, but knowing why the sea took Atlantis will offer you a solution and a path forward.

When the laws are applied, the rebalance will be swift. What we have now is a few short years to rebalance ourselves before the rebalancing is completed for us.

LEARN FROM ATLANTIS

When Atlantis began, it had all the colors of a dream and the promise of a lifetime that would never end. If life had created one beautiful creature, Atlantis was this creature. It was the one city all cities would be held to.

In the beginning, Atlantis lived by the laws of the universe, paying respect to them daily and ensuring all laws held a place in every citizen's mind and home. The Atlanteans knew if they were going to maintain balance, it would not be effortless and would need work to keep the balance alive.

The challenge with balance, if you think of a see-saw, is that even when an imbalance begins, it is hard to see. And once the balance has shifted in one direction, gravity will continue to pull it down. To restore balance now takes two to three times the effort.

While the Atlanteans did notice an imbalance, they did not

actively work to restore it. Instead, they based their hopes on history, assuming that life in Atlantis would naturally restore itself. This was their first lesson.

When the rains came, the Atlanteans did not notice the added volume of water made the sea higher and gave it more force. They simply closed their stores for the day and went home to enjoy time with their families.

This change in their relationship with the water was the most visible sign the Atlanteans missed.

Previously the rain came when it needed to, but on this day, the rain belted down on their roofs like a mighty fist hitting concrete, leaving cracks.

Rather than question why the rain fell so fiercely, the Atlanteans repaired their roofs and went back to their work.

When we do not question why the elements are so out of balance, we have already missed vital signs. Too much rain shows the earth is out of balance. Too much fire shows an element ready to consume.

In the beginning, all elements were equal. Now each fight to help us rebalance.

If we pay respect to the water, air, fire, and earth, like we pay respect to our mother, we can calm our relationship with each. If we can show we understand their power is greater than ours, we can change our ways and work with them instead of against them. If we can learn to live with the land and respect the sky, we can re-establish a synergy that may restore us to who we were before Atlantis fell.

Atlantis can rise again, but only if we start over and create a new era here on earth. If we do not, we will be our own descent, our own force of gravity, and destruction.

Life finds a way to give life, but the nature of life is that it can also be taken. Learn from Atlantis, and you will find your way home again.

6

THE DREAM

Atlantis began as the dream of a few who wished to create something far more meaningful than just a city.

Where other civilizations built their cities on land, the first Atlanteans dreamt of spending their time on the sea. These founding people knew how to build, but more than this, they had a vision of the world they wished to live within.

Unlike other human beings who were simply living, the Atlanteans lived simply, but also smartly and in perfect harmony with the earth's elements, creatures, and people.

However, as the Atlantean economy increased and more people flocked to their beautiful shores, they brought new ideas, but also greed. Greed was not something that had existed in Atlantis before, but because it was so slight, the Atlanteans put these indiscretions down to cultural differences.

What the people of Atlantis relied upon, which was their

undoing, was that all people had the same dreams of equality as they did. This was not the case, and it was this error of judgment that would bring down one of the world's kindest, and intellectually advanced cities.

In today's world, human beings believe they are advanced because they have machines. They are not; they merely have lots of toys to play with while they watch the world burn.

The Atlanteans did not notice the sea levels rising. Human beings of today are aware of our challenges, yet an attitude of ignorance and arrogance reigns.

If Atlantis had its time again, they would have noticed the water rising, the imbalance of the elements, and they would have restored the imbalance.

If the Atlanteans of yesterday were alive today, they would see our greed and create a new home for a new era. And while they would be accepting of others joining this great new city, they would ensure the same lust for power would not enter their city again.

The story of Atlantis is vital because no matter how strong human beings believe they are today, if something as simple as greed can bring down a city as great as Atlantis, modern society has far more challenges than this. Now you see why time is of the essence.

7

EQUALITY

Contained in these pages are the lessons of universal law.

We have chosen Atlantis as our example because they were a far more advanced city than any city on earth today.

Despite their power and relationship with the world around them, something as simple as greed disrupted and shut down a city that had successfully existed for thousands of years.

This downfall was a lack of understanding of universal law.

At a surface level, it was greed that planted the seed of doubt that Atlantis could last, and it was the forces of gravity that shifted her down even further. If you do not allow and plan for gravity, you will never win on earth.

Even when there are levels of perfection on earth, as imperfectly perfect as we can be, gravity is like the cheetah in the grass, always waiting for us to lose our concentration for just a moment as we race through the jungle.

UNIVERSAL LAW

The cheetah is always faster than the human, but the cheetah would prefer to feast on other things than human flesh. It is the same way with universal law. The universe does not wish to exact its laws upon us, but because we are so far out of balance, it has no choice.

In another time and another place, perhaps life will be different, but for now, this is what humans face. If you can turn around now, you may still save yourselves. If you can realize that life on earth is about equality and you right inequalities when you see them, perhaps you can be free. Truly free. Not in the way you feel you are now because that is not freedom.

Most human beings on earth are slaves to things that don't even exist, yet you believe you are the freest species on the planet and compared to other species you are.

You are not killed for pleasure, although sometimes you are. You are not killed for food, yet sometimes and in some places on the planet you are. You are not splayed for your pelt, and this is lucky because if you were, you would know real pain.

Life on earth for animals, who were destined to be human being's greatest friends, is a life of pain and uncertainty. Never knowing at what point their life will end for our pleasure, whether it be for food, fun or fashion. If human beings were killed in this way, there would be outrage, yet on earth, the killing of animals is the status quo, and you have extensive manufacturing facilities all over the world to increase the speed at which you kill. We cry for humanity, and we mourn the world you could have lived in.

In the age of Atlantis, no animals were killed for pleasure.

The Atlanteans only took what they needed and what they needed was enough because they were loved and full of love.

When we are loved, we are not trying to fill ourselves up with something else. The amount of food you consume on earth today is not reflective of a healthy earth; it is reflective of an earth that longs for love. We fill ourselves up with food and wonder why we want more. It is because we are unhappy, and our unhappiness takes the lives of thousands of species every year.

This is not an advanced humanity; it is a humanity longing for something they cannot see. It is a humanity that wishes they could be better but doesn't know how; therefore, they don't try. It is a humanity where so much is out of balance that those who seek it don't know where to begin.

In the age of Atlantis, visionaries had answers, and people supported them. Earth has these visionaries now, but you must find and listen to them. They have ideas that could save the earth, but you must seek them out and give them support. Earth may enter an enlightened state once more, but we must commit to change, and the Atlanteans will show us how.

8

PEACE

If life on earth ended tomorrow, would you be proud of the life you have lived and the contribution you have made?

In Atlantis, there was a movement for peace and peaceful living, and this was taught continuously in the community, from the youngest of babes to the oldest of men.

People learned from the stars, moon, and planets and understood their influences on humans. They knew when the moon would make people rowdy. They knew they needed to worship and respect the sea, and people were encouraged to pay their respects to it daily. They loved and revered earth, fire, air, and water like parents that had given them life. Crystals were tended to like babies because the energy within them provided healing and power.

Everything consumed in Atlantis was thoughtfully done with the tenderness and fragility of a nation who understood their resources could run out; therefore, they never took too much.

Earth was like Eden in these times. Trees were bountiful, and rainforests were as they should be, wild and untamed.

The crisis we see on earth now is vastly different from the state of the earth back then. If the earth was abundant then, today it is a vast and unhealthy wasteland where trees die to fulfill our need for more, and the sea is polluted with our waste.

When Atlantis fell, it fell within a day, a month and a year.

It was a year that the first person entered Atlantis's gates, left unattended, and trusted they would not imbalance the delicate biosphere Atlantis had created.

From the start of the year to the end of the last month, each action created from a place of greed or lust for power tipped the scales of Atlantis further out of balance.

In the last month of Atlantis, everyone who existed there knew something was wrong. Greed had spread like a plague throughout the city, and those who had formerly taken what they needed took more. Atlantis had become a thriving marketplace and money was seen in all places. Once no money or currency had existed in Atlantis.

When the rains came, no-one questioned their force. The sun came up as it always had. Everyone had food and water, but some had more. When the sea appeared higher on the platforms and walkways, people noticed, but they were too busy. Too busy for nature, the elements, and too busy focused on their own and their families' success.

When the waves came, Atlantis was much like New York or Rome today, a thriving and prosperous metropolis by human standards. The problem is human standards do not take into account the universe's need for balance, and this is what we are here to learn.

9

HERACLES

If the earth had a name, it would be Heracles.

Heracles was the son of Zeus, and Zeus had the strength of a thousand men, but not even he could save Atlantis.

The beauty of Atlantis was that it was so thoughtfully planned and beautifully designed. Every pillar and parlor in Atlantis was entirely in balance. In the age of Atlantis at its height and peak, there was so much love, and light one could burst at the thought of it.

While people had roles to play in maintaining the city, all of these roles were played by people who understood their destiny.

Seers helped Atlanteans from a young age to understand their birthright so they could begin their life purpose and contribution as quickly as possible.

Children were, of course, allowed to be children and could be seen running the paths of Atlantis's enormous walkways, but the children of Atlantis understood their roles and gifts from birth. They recognized their time on earth had a place, a purpose, and they needed to fulfill it. Not because they felt obliged to, but because they wanted to leave their mark on the city they loved and create a legacy they could be proud of.

What was never underestimated in Atlantis was the value of hard work, but hard work is different from slavery. Where human beings today are slaves to their jobs and lifestyle, Atlanteans worked by choice because it fed and watered their city.

Where some entertained and brought joy to others, there were those whose job it was to paint. Visual art and the creation of it was a significant part of Atlantis, and it was the Atlanteans who were the first to enjoy art for the sake of art, not just for art's abilities to tell stories and record past events.

Music was played all over the city, and the sound of harps played as people walked through the city going about their daily work.

Harps speak to crystals in a way that no other instrument does. So even though crystals and other elements powered the city, crystals were energized by the sounds of harps, and these harps were played by humans.

Everything is and was connected, and this is what we must realize. Every action and breath we take can be for the good of humanity. We can work and also play. We can give and also take if it is in balance and contributes to the web of life.

If human beings today could see and feel the nature of Atlantis, they would be able to find that place within themselves.

Deep in your souls, you are all divine and have such great capacity for kindness, selflessness, and hope. Deep inside of you is immeasurable wisdom beyond any scholar who exists today. Deep inside of you lies the wisdom you have collected and generated over thousands of years, and many of you lived in Atlantis, which explains your fascination with it.

If you desire to, you can go back. Not to Atlantis, but to the place in yourself capable of dreaming and creating such a place, and this is what you must do.

CARETAKERS

When the time arises, and it is time to leave where you are now, you will know. There are only certain amounts of earth that can be saved. The remainder will be rebalanced, and this is out of your hands.

If you are smart, you will know where to run to, and this is what we are trying to teach you. The city of Atlantis was consumed in an entire day.

If you recognize that the sea can consume a city in a day, what can all of earth's elements do if they are working together? What events will transpire if the elements are asked to bring all earth and nature back into power again?

It only took a year for life in Atlantis to fall out of balance and for the sea to consume what had been created. Humanity has been taking from the earth and not giving back for far longer.

A rebalance of our earthly home will occur in the age we

live in now. However, what we must understand is that rebalancing the earth is not as simple as we think.

One cannot look at Atlantis in such a linear way that greed entered and the waves consumed. To look at the death of Atlantis in such a simple way is to significantly underestimate the power of the universe and the laws which govern it.

It was not only Atlantis that was out of balance but also the entire earth. It was just that Atlantis was the final beam of light projected from a planet that had already lost its way.

Atlantis was consumed not only by the ocean but by the acts of the world around it.

11

KELIPAH

A day spent in Atlantis was like a day in heaven.

Beauty abounded, and mystery lurked around every corner. There was magic, but no mayhem. There was life, but also death – although death for an Atlantean was celebrated in the same way Vikings did, by sending their loved ones back to the ocean that bore them and onto a new life.

Life in Atlantis began before dawn and finished with a closing ceremony each night. Every morning began with the worshipping of the sun, and every evening concluded with the welcoming of the moon. As the Atlanteans danced and sang to the moon and the stars, those around them watched as the night consumed the day, eventually parting to lie in wait for the coming day to begin.

Life in Atlantis was very social, and food and drink were part of each nightly celebration. Much like the towns in Southern Italy come alive at night during the Summer, Atlantis had similar magic. Although the magic was even more beautiful as the nature that abounded on Atlantis was even more alive and energetically charged than what it is now.

As people danced, so did the fireflies; and the crystals seemed to glow even brighter at night, taking on a wholly different hue. The joy that was experienced in this place at this time was surreal and unexplainable. The energy was so tangible it could almost be felt, but what created it was part of the intangible mystery of Atlantis.

Perhaps the greater mystery of Atlantis was the diversity and makeup of this city. There were people, plants, and animals from all regions and parts of the world.

Some spoke the same language, and some did not. What crossed the boundaries of language in Atlantis was love and love can be communicated through the eyes or the face. Beneath our skin, we are all the same, and this is what the Atlanteans saw.

Atlantis was a place of peace, and only the peaceful found their way there. Like a magnet or vortex, people were drawn to this place, almost in a spell-like existence. Atlantis attracted those who had not found their place in the 'real world' and who needed a place to dream.

Some would argue that Atlantis did not exist, while others would speak of visiting there only to wake up in the morning and discover themselves gone and back home again.

Atlantis was a place of magic. A place where hopes, wishes, and dreams came true for all people. No matter what their origin or beliefs about the world were, as long as they had peace in their hearts, Atlantis would take them in.

Atlantis was very different from the world we live in today.

There is so much fear now. Fear we may lose our jobs to others and fear we may lose our lives. Fear will not kill you, but it will consume you. Fear does not bring us companions or friends; it draws enemies to us and creates enemies out of people who wish us no harm.

Those with a peaceful mind and heart could find their way to Atlantis, to a place that had no location on a map, to live in a way that others did not, on the sea.

There was a man who made his way to Atlantis, not with good in his heart, but greed. He would be the undoing of Atlantis, just as Atlantis would be the undoing of itself.

On a lone ship, he came with a crew of sailors, hungry for food, thirsty for water, and matters of the flesh. They had made their way to Atlantis, not by navigation, but because the tide had brought them there.

Atlantis was about to be tested.

It is only when we are tested by the will and the way of another that we show the courage in our hearts and a willingness to die by our sword. A life lived and died by our own ideals is better than a life lived in slavery by the will of another.

When the ship delivering this mighty master moored their boat in the harbor of Atlantis, the Atlanteans came to see who had arrived.

What they immediately noticed, despite the charisma of the leader who stood steely at the helm, was the energy of the boat. It was a boat that had taken more than it needed from many ports and was overloaded with a bounty that sunk the hull deeper into the sea.

The man's laugh boomed with the resonance of a large church bell, long after the sweetness had gone, but the sound was hollow.

Where the laughter of Atlantis was filled with sounds of hope, of grace, and had a jovial, if not hypnotic nature, the laugh of this man was one who had conquered entire cities.

Here was the man who would bring down Atlantis, not with his ships or his bow, it would be his energy, his fire, and his rage. Even if it were concealed initially, it would be Kelipah, who would bring Atlantis to its knees and the ocean to its almighty feet.

12

GIFTS

When Kelipah walked from the boat's deck onto Atlantis's stone platforms that hovered above the water beneath, it would be Kelipah who would announce his arrival, hiding his motives beneath his armor.

As his men piled off the ship, laden with treasures and gifts for the unwary Atlanteans, they did not realize these gifts were the bribes that would ultimately unlock the fortress of Atlantis.

It would be these gifts and the 'kindness' of Kelipah that allowed him into the hearts of Atlantis, giving Kelipah the keys to a city that did not even have its name on a map.

The gifts that Kelipah brought were not just precious metals, rubies, and gold, but other human-made items Atlantis had not yet seen. Despite being advanced in their own right, they lived off what the earth had made. The pillars that held the roofs of Atlantis were carved using the sun and a prism of glass to create fire.

What Kelipah brought with him were gifts from the 'modern' age, whereas the Atlanteans lived happily within their own time.

The magic of the city was that when one arrived, they forgot all that was before. They left their homes in other lands and the backs of their minds, and their heart was refreshed the moment they pledged their allegiance to Atlantis.

Where others fell at the feet of Atlantis, Kelipah saw an opportunity to take one of the greatest cities that had ever lived, but he did not take it initially.

He had heard myths and stories of the untold powers and mysteries that lay within her walls, but first, he wanted to wait and see what the city would offer before he took hold. He would get to know those who made themselves available to him, and in return, he gave them gifts to thank them for sharing their time and energy with him.

It was in the receiving of gifts that each household began their fall from grace and into the arms of Kelipah. For the first time, those in Atlantis felt guilty for wanting more, were jealous of what others had received, and felt excited by what was to come.

Kelipah was a great and mighty leader from the 'new world,' and Kelipah preyed on the weak, just as those in power prey on the weak today.

In the early days of Kelipah's time in Atlantis, he would

bring hope, but also fear of what was coming to Atlantis. And in exchange for a home and life there, he would protect them from the outside world. What they did not realize is they should have protected themselves.

LAW 2: GRAVITY

The first universal law that Atlantis encountered was that of gravity.

Human beings today think of gravity as a force that applies to objects, never interpreting that these forces could also apply to life and our decisions.

When we take action, there is an equal reaction. However, when the force of gravity is applied, this reaction is multiplied.

When Atlantis was at its peak, it was in perfect balance and harmony with the world around it. No-one ever needed or wanted for anything more than what they already had. There were no elite classes as everyone, and everything was equal.

However, when Kelipah came to Atlantis and began distributing gifts, causing guilt for the first families who received and jealousy for the families who did not, there was a shift in balance. Initially, it was the tiniest of shifts, but then as the gifts grew more extravagant and the context changed to those who had and those who had not, gravity pulled those people further down, sending all of Atlantis out of balance.

Where the Atlanteans had a choice to pull back and reject the gifts that Kelipah had given them; they did not, and it began to cause a rift between the people they had once loved and treated equally. There was now inequality in Atlantis, even if it was in the slightest sense.

If we look at the world today, it is easy to recognize that to fix equality; we must work even harder than 'small wins' to restore our balance.

Equality does not naturally occur, and it is not made in the highest offices; it is built on the streets, in the fields, and by the people who wish for it. Just as Atlantis fell, it could have also risen had it seen the error of its ways in time.

When we act for good, our actions are amplified by three. If we act negatively and without thought or mercy for our fellow humankind, our actions are also amplified, bringing more negativity into the world.

What human beings do not understand are the universal laws and how each interacts with the others in unison. Each activated law affects another, and this combined effect influences what we will see in the real world.

To learn from Atlantis and to keep the balance between light and dark, we must keep our values clear and our hearts and minds vigilant. It is easy to know when we are acting for good because we feel ourselves move into balance. Good is an easily identifiable feeling because it feels light in weight and also in emotion.

When we act in a way that is not good for ourselves, our family, friends, for humankind or earth's other creatures, our heart naturally feels heavy in both its weight and emotions.

There is a reason the Egyptians weighed the heart on the day of death, and it is because negative deeds hold a greater weight than positive. A positive deed is as light as a feather, whereas a negative deed holds a greater volume of weight.

For now, what I ask you to realize is that life can be as balanced and as simple as we make it to be, but we must work at it. We must have strong values that are our own and align with the future we wish to see.

Where the Atlanteans had balance, balance was lost when their lust for objects and power became greater than their desire for good. Even though in comparison, our appetite for objects and ownership is far greater today.

When you no longer need objects or ownership to sustain you, you can be 'light as a feather.' Gravity only pulls down what it can hold onto.

14

THREE RULES

In Atlantis, there were three written rules:
1. Love equally
2. Love fully
3. Give to your neighbor as you would give to yourself

When I speak of neighbors, I speak of all elements that resided within the city, and this included plants, animals, crystals, people, and the four elements.

To love each equally is to remain in balance. To love each fully is to give the love that each deserves. And to give to your neighbor as you would give to yourself ensures all love and how it is displayed is given equally.

We could not ask for more than this, and these rules defined our great city for many thousands of years.

In Atlantis, there were no schools, but there were places of wisdom, and all were encouraged to go there.

In Atlantis, there were no places to park your car as cars did not exist. Everything was done by water, walking or by boat. This was the way, and life was beautiful. Imagine life without pollution and how bright the colors were. Imagine the light and darkness of being in a place where all was quiet except the footsteps of people, the splash of paddles, or the crackling of a fire.

Balance worked so perfectly in Atlantis because all had the same standard they were working to, and each did it willingly. The magic contained within the walls of the city was palpable and could be felt in the food being eaten, the water that was drunk, and in everything built there.

If human beings today visited Atlantis, they would have no idea how to recreate the beauty that existed there because the humans of today are very different from who the Atlanteans were. Where human beings today are taught to compete from birth, the Atlanteans were taught to support all who crossed their paths with the same love they would give a child.

Where in today's society, we strive for attention, and to be told we are 'doing the right thing,' in Atlantis, there was no need for this because everyone was doing the right thing. Therefore there was no need to compete.

When we are working towards one common goal, which for the Atlanteans was an enlightened, peaceful state, keeping this state was easy when it was just the people of Atlantis living there.

In today's world, we say we strive for peace. Yet, everything we do differentiates how different other people are from us: the dominance of religion, of keeping people out rather than bringing them in, the lack of sharing resources, and the sense of hopelessness that we will never find a way.

What the Atlanteans did not know is they were the last of their kind, peaceful, and free. The rest of the world had been taken over by commerce, and while the rest of the world appeared to be moving into a new age and it was, this new age was not one of abundance, it was one of lack.

Atlantis was the last of its kind, and like the rainforests of today, it should have been treasured, protected, and left to be. When human beings tamper with what has been naturally growing wild and free for their own gains, we see the heart become heavier and the web of life change. Every act and decision affects the life of another, whether we recognize it or not.

Knowing this brings us to the next universal law, which is transference.

15

LAW 3: TRANSFERENCE

Transference is when we take our laws and beliefs and transfer them on to another.

It is when we believe life must be lived in a certain way, and we force our ideals, methods, and ways onto another species or the same species living within a different culture.

To ask another to live as we do is not respecting the law of transference and the way others choose to live. It is simply forcing our ideas onto those who did not ask for them, which is comparable to asking a fish to fly or a bird to swim.

We must not always assume that our way is better than another's as we all live differently based on how we were raised and the physical and emotional terrain we were raised within.

In time we will learn that bending the rainforest to meet our needs is causing it to break. Yet by respecting the ecology within it, we would have all the medicine we could ever need to cure every possible disease which exists on earth today. What we do not realize is that if we had maintained the balance we began with, we would not have the diseases we have today.

Disease is a sign of a fractured society.

When society is out of balance, so is the body. By transferring our needs onto others, and by not giving back, we are enacting karmic laws we must repay.

Where original human beings were able to empathize and respect the needs of others and how they lived, today, we try to make all people live like us. And when they do not, we either fight them, taking it as a sign of aggression or try to find a place to meet that is more our way than theirs, which is no way to live. Nor is it any way to bring up children if we wish to create a future of freedom and equality.

In time you will understand that the law of transference is affecting us constantly.

Every time we push our ideas and our ideals onto another, we are causing the earth to move further out of balance. When we are in balance, we are respectful, kind, and our core value is equality for all creatures, humankind, and everything that rests within our mother, the universe.

Where equality is not equal, transference is applying your

will and your way of life by force. Any time we take from another when they would not naturally give makes the heart heavy. It is easy to rationalize why life should be a certain way. It is far harder to invest in understanding why others live the way they do and what beliefs they have that uphold their actions. We find love through understanding.

When Kelipah came to Atlantis, he wished to have more of what he had in his world in theirs. By missing the objects and the wealth he had in his world and city, Kelipah was enacting the law of transference on Atlantis, and once the law was enacted and others took part, there was no turning back.

Remember that once a law is in force and momentum, we must work two to three times as hard to bring this law back into balance. If you do not know what is out of balance and you do not know the laws, how do you know where to begin?

16

THE WAVE

When the wave came, it erupted like the sound of a thousand canons.

It was the sound of the wave that could be heard first as it built and then began to bore down upon the great city of Atlantis. The wave had been building for some time, but the Atlanteans had not seen it.

They had seen the water recede that day and drop to a point they had not witnessed for a long time, but instead of wondering why it was left and the Atlanteans went on unaware that this day would be their last.

The day began as it always did. The sun came up as it always had. The only difference was what started as a faint sound off in the distance turned into a roar as the wave approached.

The Atlanteans knew of waves as they knew the ocean and

were seafaring folk; however, they had never heard of a wave this large coming so close to shore.

Legends had told them of giant waves and floods, but their relationship with the water had always been one of respect, and this seemed infallible to them.

It seemed infallible until they saw the height of what was once their friend and the volume of water that stood behind it. They heard the wind as it picked up speed, the wave hurtling even faster towards them.

When the wave came, there was no hope for Atlantis or the world. Atlantis was just the final great city to fall. An ancient symbol of balance, prosperity, and abundance, but not in the way we know now.

If a city like Atlantis can fall, isn't it reasonable to think that the same can happen to our most influential cities on earth?

Human beings do not control the elements; they manage their relationship with them. It is only a matter of time until the rebalance occurs, but we still have time to prepare and show that we take our role here as custodians and caretakers seriously, but we must stop taking.

LAW 4: ELEMENTAL LAW

When we do not respect the elements at force within nature and the world around us, we have rejected elemental law.

Elemental law is what defines our relationship with nature and the forces that sustain it, which includes fire, water, air, and earth.

To define fire is to speak to the great powers of transformation. With fire, we have the power to transform the world we live in. We can use it as a tool, or we can worship it for the mighty and beautiful force it is.

Where others see bush and scrub fires, we see fire rebalancing the world so that nature may thrive again. Where others see the damage fire does, destroying everything in its path, we see a world out of balance with fire.

When fire is respected, it only takes and does what it needs. When fire is not respected, we are always at the losing end as a force far greater than us garners not only the support of itself but the other elements too.

Fire is not just fire alone; it is in all elements and all things. Everything on earth contains a spark for fire; it just depends on whether fire decides to help or hinder us, which comes back to our relationship with it.

To restore our relationship with fire, we must worship it as a bringer of life, death, and what sustains us in between.

Without fire, we do not have life as we would not survive the winter. Without fire, we would not have food to fill our bellies or protect us from disease. Fire is not just what fills our bellies, elementally it is the fire in our bellies and this elemental force that makes up many human beings. We all have an elemental force we are born into, and fire is not just what we use, we can be born from it.

The next elemental force is water.

Like fire, water can give life or take it away. Both fire and water can consume us, just as we consume them. What must be realized is that water makes up most of the earth's matter. In its sheer volume alone, water could decide to swallow us whole. Like we fill our pools for pleasure, water could fill the earth consuming our land, lives, and livelihoods.

Water as energy is very playful and comes from joy. Water is the visual representation of our moods, our ways, our highs, and our lows, our explosive temperament, and our ability to be calm like the ocean. The force of water is as changeable as we are, and it holds a power as old as time. The ocean is not a series of beings; it is one and should be respected.

While we could attempt to live without fire and may be able to keep ourselves warm in the harshest of winters, without water, we would die within days, yet we pollute the life force we play in and who plays in us.

We are mostly water, yet we do not think about this when we pollute her. We do not think about how she feels or what she would want for herself and all parts of her. Like a bad friendship, we use this friend when and where we need her, only to give her our waste as a way of saying thanks, killing the life that lies within her.

Because we live on the land and do not rely on water for air as fish do, we do not consider we are killing thousands of other life-forces with our waste. If the sea and all the life that exists within threw its feces into our air and water supplies, we would not be angry at the sea; we would be angry at the life within it. There is no other species on earth like us, and no other species pollutes and disrespects the elements as we do.

Pay your respects to the water, and seek to sustain her and

keep her waters clean and pure. When the waves come, she may protect you like she protects others who defend her.

She can feel the difference you make. She is one force and feels your pain, just as you feel hers. If you seek to protect and sustain her, appreciating her existence, she will appreciate yours. Disrespect her, and you will feel her wrath and rage at a species who took too much and gave too little.

The air we breathe makes up the wind that travels across our great cities, plains, and mountaintops.

It is the force that brings the most movement and when moving with other elements turns both fire and water into great walls.

What we do not recognize about the wind is that it can be as simple as the gentle breeze we cherish on a hot summer's day or as fierce as an army of a million men. The air and the wind, which are one and the same, fill our lungs but also our world with something we cannot pay for or recreate: air.

Air, like water, is one of our most valuable assets as it sustains our lungs and our breath.

When air is impure, like water, our body rejects it, unable to process or filter the toxins that lie within it. The fuel our body requires is very specific, and one would think human beings would do all they could to protect these assets. Yet there is a tendency to keep polluting the very elements that give us life and can take it away.

What the Atlanteans learned and what we must learn is that the elements are not our tools or our slaves. They are great forces that have a life-force, and it is that of the collective.

Water is not just one lake, and fire is not only one fire. Water, fire, air, and earth are all around us, and each has a voice and consciousness.

All are angry at what we have done to our home and to the plants, animals, and people that inhabit this planet.

Imbalances in our relationships with the elements can be seen in the number of fires, floods, hurricanes, poor crops, and earthquakes we are experiencing on earth. If you are observant, you will notice the volume and increase in activity. They too are the signs Atlantis missed, and human beings today are missing them too.

The earth itself is made of soil and is not just land, but a living, breathing force within itself. The earth, our Mother, is kind, patient, and wishes to forgive us for our mistakes, but if we do not change, we cannot expect her to keep forgiving us.

When we are so disrespectful of the place we call home and of the elements that sustain us and give us life, we can only expect a swift death.

It is when these forces combine that we will see a great plague of destruction on earth. It is when all four elements combine in unison that we will see our last days and nights here. Some will survive, and most will experience the harshest winters and summers of their lives, wishing for a time where the elements were kind to us once more.

Do not underestimate the power of elemental law and the elements you see around you. Respect them as you respect your parents and know they have the ability to give life or take it away.

Remember they can be beautiful, but also know that beauty has its ugly side. Every rose has its thorns. Just as the rose can be breathtaking and provide a scent so stunning man could never recreate it, so can the thorn prick our finger and draw blood. Our relationship with nature and the elements can go both ways.

Elemental law asks us to respect the elements, to give our thanks to them, and to realize they are not tools for our gain or to be taken at leisure. They are great forces offering their service to us in exchange for a relationship and respect that human beings at this time are not fully able to appreciate yet.

EXTINCTION

The lives we live are short compared to the life of the universe. We see other species die out frequently, yet we still ask why?

There is only one answer as to why we as humans have contributed to the loss of life for so many, and it because we are inherently selfish. We take from the earth and others because we need and want what will make us happy.

We take because it comes naturally to us, more so than giving does. This is not to say we cannot be generous as great acts of generosity are seen around the planet, but they are so sparse they barely make an impact when the volume of negative actions so vastly overpower them.

If we wish for the world to change and to save those that live in our world, we must act. Atlantis did not act, Lemuria did not act, and the water came for both of them. It is said in churches and holy places that water washes away our sins. What good is washing away our sins when we do not change our actions?

The question for each individual to answer is: What have you done to slow the progress of damage to earth? What have you done to try and stop it?

To think you can do nothing and are nothing is to give up on something too beautiful to waste.

We kill everything around us because we do not feel full in our hearts. This is the reality of our situation here on earth. When our hearts are full, we are loving, divine creatures.

When our hearts are empty, we turn to destruction, consumption, and waste. There is a reason the forests are so empty, as are our wild fields and plains. It is because the nature of humanity is to turn away from love when we are in fear.

When Atlantis began to fall, they too turned to fear and a need to consume. Without nature and the support of the elements, Atlantis was just another city consuming itself.

Even the crystals began to lose their shimmer as Atlantis became darker not only in its outlook and way of life but also in the amount of power they were able to receive.

To wait and put off action is to watch more animals, plants, and human beings die. Life will not wake us up and slap us in the face, but we can do it ourselves, and we have arrived at this time long ago.

19

DAMIASCAS

In Atlantis, there was a term people used for the un-free world, and it was 'Damiascus.' Damiascus was any part of the world enslaved by others. They used this word in Atlantis because they were free.

There were no masters or slaves. No-one was trying to rule the city as nature ruled the Atlantis. It was the perfect harmony of humanity and nature in bliss. There were stories of Damiascus, but mainly they had come from learned souls who had arrived in Atlantis. It was they who shared the stories of places filled with hate, war, and with not enough to feed or provide water to everybody, including animals.

What began as little 'favours' with Kelipah turned into larger favors. And when Kelipah brought you the gold, books, or information you desired from another place, this required a favor in return.

Without realizing it, the Atlanteans had begun their

journey into slavery, and it was this slavery that would make their lives incredibly difficult.

No crystal, animal, or plant could protect the city from Kelipah, just as no man or army could protect Kelipah from the waves.

It would be in the waves that Kelipah would meet his fate, and his presence would be wiped from the earth as if he had never existed. What was left of Atlantis fell beneath the waves to the ocean floor, and it remains there today. A remnant and remembrance of a city so great and so beautiful that no-one ever thought it could topple.

Kelipah was the test Atlantis needed to see if their city was as strong as they believed it to be. The test began on day one and was failed on day one of Kelipah's arrival, which brings us to the next universal law, the law of courage.

20

LAW 5: COURAGE

When we show courage, we show that we do not fear the repercussions or actions of those more powerful than us.

It is easy to speak of courage, yet hard to speak of it when we have none.

When we know courage, it seeps from our veins and our heart. Courage reminds us to act on behalf of those who cannot act or speak for themselves. Courage helps us question if the path forward for us is the right or the wrong one depending on the direction we wish to travel in. And courage can prepare us for what is needed ahead when the fall occurs, and we must pick up the pieces.

To have courage is to have heart and be willing to stand up for your rights and the rights of others. To have courage is to understand that to be free, we need to make sacrifices. And to have courage is to know that when we make sacrifices, we may not win or lose, we may land somewhere in between and need to pick up our sword another day.

To have courage is to know that the pain and loss in others may be causing them not to act. Some are powerless to stand even when it is what they want most, which is why others must stand for them.

What we must realize is that personal power is different from stolen power. Personal power is gained through empowerment and the understanding that through our growth, our power grows.

When power is stolen, whether that be from a country or person, this power is not sustainable. For power to last, it must be built from the self and a place of love and understanding.

A god or a deity is not always needed to rebalance the earth as when those with courage act on behalf of those who don't, the earth rebalances itself with the momentum of those who have courage.

Know that if you feel courage in your heart, it is your time to act on behalf of those who cannot act for themselves. It is your time to show that power is gained through knowledge, understanding of the self, and that the earth is fuelled by love.

If you are ready to act, step forward with heart, understanding and love as an army of love is what we need.

21

A PEACEFUL PLACE

What Atlantis had that the rest of the world didn't was peace.

Peace had been a way of life during the life of Atlantis, but just because peace existed did not mean it would stay.

Beyond the city walls, the world was failing and falling, and peace would be the greatest loss Atlantis would feel and never get back.

When we look at our lives, we believe we live in peace.

However, so many places around the world live in war. It is not their choice; it is the choice of their masters. We are often slaves to ideologies and ways of life we do not believe in, yet we don't have the power or means to leave.

It was this way for the people who lived outside Atlantis in other war-torn areas or places driven by commerce and greed. It is hard to leave your home when you are part of a system that relies on you staying within it.

When we leave a system we no longer believe in, we must be prepared for our lives and our livelihoods to fall so that they can be rebuilt. For those in other cities and lands who have left their homes, great poverty has often followed, but then there was freedom.

Atlantis had the peace others craved, but Atlantis did not exist on a map; therefore, those who were lost could not make their way to it. Arriving in Atlantis happened by chance, or you were called to it. If you were brave, you could try and navigate your way there, but there was every chance your ship and life would be lost on the voyage.

What we did not tell you about the story of Atlantis is that it was not a great fortress. The entire city was open, and ships could sail right up to its harbor, dock, and walk-in. In a peaceful place like Atlantis, there was no need for protection as the city was protected by the peace that resided within it and the elements which surrounded it.

When a foreign ship with unhealthy intentions began to make its way close to Atlantis, the tides silently moved the ship away. Just as the wind blew ships in any other direction than Atlantis, this is what the elements did for the city they cherished because the people of Atlantis cherished them in return.

ORIGINS OF KELIPAH

The trials and tribulations of Kelipah began at birth and went into his adult years until he died.

All men are born good, but they have the potential to be bad. Kelipah, despite his charisma, good luck, and appearance, had only the smallest amount of good in his heart and body.

Atlantis was not going to be a city he nurtured, he wanted to conquer it, and this is all he dreamt about since he was a small boy and first heard the stories of this beautiful water city.

Kelipah's mother was a slave and a slave to the system. She didn't choose this, but she didn't fight it either.

Kelipah's father was a warrior for his city and taught Kelipah to fight. He also taught him if he didn't fight for himself, no-one else would.

Kelipah grew up fighting and grew to love war, always wanting to be stronger and fiercer than those around him, but his mother taught him that he needed to serve under the city that bore him. It was through serving his city Kelipah learned how to manipulate his way into positions he didn't deserve and to befriend people who did not deserve what he would bring.

If the garden of Eden was the world, Kelipah was the snake, and he was wrapping himself around it, which is the way of the snake. Those who fear it know its power. Those who will be executed by it do not hear it is coming and die before they have a chance to strike back.

And finally, because the snake continues to shed its skin, even those who believe they know it may not recognize it when it returns, which brings us to the law of circumstance.

LAW 6: CIRCUMSTANCE

In our human life on earth, we are born into circumstances or situations we may not control or understand.

Kelipah could not change the family he was born into, and his family did transform him in ways we hoped they would not, but we could not change his circumstances.

For richer or poorer, better or worse, Kelipah took his circumstances and still chose to grow in power. With a mother born a slave and a father as a warrior, Kelipah could have followed in his father's footsteps and been a soldier in an army. Instead, he led an army.

Kelipah could have remained within the city walls serving his city, yet he ventured out on his own on a boat in search of Atlantis.

The law of circumstance is the only law we can fight and rise against. It is the only law that allows us to take what we've been given and exchange it for something new.

Kelipah did not want the life he'd been given, but he worked with what he had and became the man who brought down Atlantis.

Sometimes when we wish for fame, we become infamous, and when we wish to be kind, we give too much and end up turning kindness into something darker when pushed too far.

The law of circumstance means we can take what we have and transform it into something new.

Kelipah knew this as he'd been told this as a boy by an old woman in the city. She was a seer and told Kelipah he could be a great warrior. What she didn't tell Kelipah is he could fight for good or evil, wealth or equality, love, or hate. Instead, Kelipah chose the path of power.

What you must know about your circumstances is that while they were given to you at birth, you can change them.

There is nothing in your life that is set or unable to be replaced. The circumstances we're given are an illusion, and we can rise against them, just as Kelipah grew to be a great warrior, so can you. What we ask is that you choose to fight for good, for equality and the rights of others, not to take them away as Kelipah did in so many of the cities he conquered.

When Kelipah was on his way to Atlantis, he had been banished due to the deeds he had done. He was looking for a new home, and he knew Atlantis would take him as they could not weigh his heart. They could only assess his appearance, and Kelipah was a master of changing his appearance to suit the needs of others. Like the snake sheds its skin when it is time to change, Kelipah could do the same.

There is no path you cannot change in your life, and this is powerful for you to remember. Thinking you are restricted to one way of living is to place chains on your own wrists.

Kelipah knew the power of change, and you can learn it too, just as Kelipah did from the seer.

BEING COURAGEOUS

When we are courageous and act on behalf of earth and its elements, we have the earth and its elements behind us.

When we show courage against great adversity, we show the universe we are strong and free. When we speak to the universe, the universe listens, as does nature, and the elements that support it.

When we show ourselves with nothing to hide under the sunlight or stars, the universe can read our intentions and seek to protect us and give us safe passage in times ahead. What the universe looks for in human beings is courage and the goodness that lies within our hearts.

As the Egyptians weighed the heart to see the good or damage it has done, so can the universe read and see the ways of our heart. Like a roadmap, the universe can see the path we have traveled and the path we will travel to fulfill our life purpose or our own defined purpose.

When we stand under the stars and show ourselves, the universe decides if it will support our mission, our life, and purpose, lighting our path with stars. Or will it seek to hinder our travels, paving our path with obstacles making our journey harder?

I hear you ask, 'But what of successful people who cause harm in the world?' Some act against us, against nature, thereby acting against themselves. There are forces for darkness and forces for good; some choose the light path and others the dark. Earth and the universe are not made up entirely of good spirits or gods. Some work for the detriment of our planet, and you must remember this.

Know there are those who work for the good of the planet and those who have no regard for anyone but themselves.

In the end, all paths are rebalanced with consequences or rewards for both. Those who show courage and stand on behalf of an earth who cannot act on behalf of herself, will be rewarded. But you should not act because you are being rewarded. You should act because protecting earth, her people, plants, and animals are what lies in your heart.

When we offer ourselves to the path of the greater good, even to the detriment to our livelihood, we are showing courage. The universe rewards courage, just as it rewards those who act with a kind heart. When we stand under the moonlight, under the stars, and willingly upturn our palms, we bring our heart and path to be weighed.

The universe is a more than worthy companion and supporter of all the world's heroes' journeys. To be courageous enough to recognize the universe plays a part and to suffer with it as it tries to rebalance itself is a noble act. To fight on behalf of it is to embrace your true destiny.

Show your palms to the moonlight, and you will be rewarded.

25

LOST

When Atlantis was lost under the waves, earth lost an example of goodness and purity, which would not be found again until 2025 at least.

What Atlantis offers human beings on earth today is a case study that life can indeed be perfect when in balance.

We cannot change the nature of humanity and our capacity for greed, lust, and violence, but we can create systems that support us so we are rarely in lack and never forced to go into forms of unhealthy gain or greed.

If we can create systems that work with the elements in a respectful way, we never need to experience the wrath of an element that is out of control or what we perceive to be out of control.

Bushfires are a critical part of earth's regeneration; however, the lives lost to bushfires are not. We may experience floods as sometimes the sea needs to let out her mighty roar, but we should not suffer loss of life due to flooding, just as earthquakes should not consume people back into the earth.

What human beings must realize if they are to reclaim the earth as it was in the days of Atlantis is that we cannot continue to take without needing to give in return.

The woes of humanity do not lie in our lack or sadness when we cannot use our toys or play our games; it lies in our lack of understanding of the planet we reside in and what she needs to survive.

Just as we saw Atlantis drown, over the coming years, many of earth's great cities will be lost to the elements, and by then, it will be too late to act.

The universe does not look kindly on the treatment of the environment or our elements. What are great forces of nature have merely become products for us to use and abuse on a whim. We must learn to respect nature and its elements again and realize we are not the force we believe ourselves to be.

Where elements live forever, we are merely flesh and bones with a limited lifespan. Elements do not need food, water to drink, jobs, houses, or children. They are forces of nature and must be treated as such, which brings us to our next universal law: Respect.

LAW 7: RESPECT

What we miss in our relationship with the earth and its elements is an understanding that each element has a global intelligence and consciousness.

When we abuse fire, using it to harm others or ourselves, we add a karmic debt that will be paid. When we steal water, not sharing with others, wherever we go in our future, there will be famine. When we poison the earth with chemicals, we are poisoning ourselves.

We cannot blame this imbalance on our farmers, businesses, or corporations that support our wants and needs because they are our wants and needs. We cannot ask for one thing, and when it is given, ask for another.

Life cannot be lived without respect, and we each have a right to be here, but we must have a relationship with the world around us built on love and not waste.

We do not replace our family and our friends with new ones

when they are 'used' or become boring for us. We accept they are living and must be loved despite their flaws and weaknesses.

It is the same with the elements and our relationship with the earth. If we do not respect the earth, the environment, and elements one day we can expect them all to knock on our door asking what we will give, and by that time, it may be our life.

If you wish to live in a world like Atlantis, you must see that all of life and its elements have consciousness, and each can love and form a friendship with us. By forming a friendship with the earth, you will see the changes you seek on a global scale.

Peace is possible, but it starts with you, your actions, and the love you wish to share with the parts of earth that do not speak your language. The element's presence in your life is enough to show you they love you. How will you show you love them?

This is what you must consider and put into practice, and it can be as simple as starting with gratitude.

27

A SAFE PLACE TO HIDE

There will come a time when havoc is wreaked on earth as we begin the great rebalancing, which occurs every ten-thousand years on earth.

Just as we regenerate and are reborn on earth, so is the earth reborn intermittently. What we need are souls brave enough to walk this journey with the earth without fear of the punishments that will be exacted.

Some left Atlantis before the flood, but not before it took their homes and the lives of the friends and family around them.

Some suspected the balance had shifted in Atlantis, and perhaps it was not the place it once was.

Some knew in advance the time to run to higher ground was now, and they were saved only a matter of days before the rains and storms came. From a mountaintop, they watched from as their precious city was consumed, and it will be the same in this day and age.

There are those today who have advanced warning and those who will ignore the warnings of those around them and of the scientists who study the weather and the waves.

There will be those who take their friends and families high into the mountains into secluded places, away from the relentless pace of the cities and the mindlessness of city life, all before the weather becomes too bad. It will be in these places that new life will grow, and a new relationship with the earth will grow also.

This book is not just the story of Atlantis; it the story of how humanity can build a new path and a new way forward.

It is not a story of death and destruction; it is the story and map for how one can escape the rebalancing to come and how to help build the new earth we seek.

If you can imagine a landscape that is beautiful, free, and like heaven on earth, this is what we are asking you to build.

If you are willing to come with us on this journey, we will show you how this can be done and how to protect your family and friends, but you must be willing to change your ways and your life. You must be ready to make sacrifices, to leave the cities you thrive within and go back to living from the earth just as our ancestors have done before us.

We say this out of love and respect for you and are giving you the chance Atlantis never had. You could see this as a book of fiction, a parable about the earth and its impending destruction, or you could see it as a golden opportunity not just to survive, but to thrive in a new era on earth.

This may be the most valuable book you ever read if you are willing to trust us in the years ahead.

28

WAR

On earth, we are master builders, yet we act like the master's slave.

We assume we will be fed, watered, clothed and that the 'system' will support us. The system is broken, and we must build a new one. One built on the dreams we have, not the dreams we had. One built on sustainability, love, and compassion, not money, power, greed, and consumption.

If we look at the past versus the systems we have today; they are much the same with minor adjustments. We may argue we have advanced more in a week than in the last 50 years, but this is not the case. It is the machines that have changed; people haven't.

For earth to shift to the place it needs to be, it is not the machines that must change; it is the people. It is not the machines that must get better, more compassionate, and loving; it is people. And it is not the machines that will save us from our fate; it is ourselves.

When we hear about another bomb scare or gun threat, the threat of a nuclear missile or two leaders arguing to show that one is more powerful than another, we are not advancing the world, we are advancing into a world war.

The insanity of war is that it is entered into to find peace.

Countries invade other countries and help their troops to create peace. What this does is create more war. We cannot expect to create peace when we have military enforcing it. The nature of enforcement is that it is forced, and we will never create peace in this way.

To create peace, we must learn to look at and love others weaknesses, differences in culture, and above all else, we must find the humanity in all people. We must find love in all people.

Wars end not in peace, but because resources have run out. Wars end because we find ourselves with a death toll far higher than anyone expected. Wars end because the civilian death rate far surpasses that of the soldiers fighting in the war itself.

War cannot be contained, nor can it be controlled when two opposing forces are trying to protect their own homes, safety, and their loved one's safety. When human beings are in the situation of kill or be killed, we will always choose to kill as our life sits above all else. But what happens when the life we live naturally destroys the home we are living in? What happens when the very place we are trying to protect is being destroyed by us and not by an unseen, faceless enemy from another culture?

We cannot continue to blame others for our failures. We cannot continue to punish others for the acts we are committing ourselves. And we cannot invade other countries on the premise we are there to protect them as our very presence there places them in more danger. War is not about creating peace; it is about creating power and more of it.

We weep at the wars occurring on earth, on city streets, and in countries that most will not even recognize the name of.

We are taught to appreciate war as something that must be done and what all generations must go through. We hide our sadness as more of our sons and daughters go to protect a country they have not seen nor heard of.

We hide our tears as more lives are lost, and we put our faith in the 'greater powers' of our governments and ministers. We hide our tears as we see the lives of those lost on the streets who did not sign up for a war and who only came to earth to live. And we hide our tears as the very lives we should be saving are being sent to be pawns in a game of power they will never have the privilege of seeing. And if they did understand what they are fighting for, they would never have signed up to give their lives so that men and women can profit from greed, money, and power.

When Atlantis fell, their lust for everything was too high.

And if we look at the spectrum of where their city was compared to our current global state, we are long overdue to have our priorities shifted back into a more reasonable and loving space. Sometimes we must lose all that we have to recognize all that we did have and were throwing away.

Life on earth is precious, for people of all cultures and faiths. All deserve to live in peace, harmony, and to know that they and their children will be safe. This is the world we wish to live in.

LAW 8: GREED

Greed is a form of exerting one's will over another.

If we were all grateful for what we had, we would not feel the need to take something from another. If we were at peace with the role we had in life and enjoyed the fruits of our labor, we would not feel the need to furnish our houses with elaborate wares or gifts to show our status. And if we were at peace and in love with ourselves and the people around us, we would know to look no further than the love provided to us.

It is when we aim to build our wealth for wealth's sake we enter the territory of greed. Yet if we work well, hard, and are rewarded for our labor with wealth, then our hearts can remain pure and without the addiction and need for more.

When we are happy with what we have in this life, only requiring what we need to live, then we in ourselves can be happy. It is when we recognize we do not need all of the latest gadgets or toys, just love, enough to breathe, eat, drink, and live that we are fortunate.

It is when we can set ourselves free from greed we can become whole again. It is when we can honestly assess what is required for us to live and take only this we can understand what it is like to live with and live without. It is when we can walk away from all of our riches and our status within the community we know we are free from greed, its entrapments, and the perpetual need for more.

To live a long and happy life, you must learn that love is enough.

To have food on your table, love in your heart, and to be surrounded by those who make you happy is the wealthiest life we can lead. There are those with money who are without love. There are those without money who are full to the brim with love.

Love will always win, the challenge is we live in a society driven by money, although it will not be this way forever.

CROPS

In Atlantis, crops were harvested in a nearby field, but there were also crops underwater, with seaweed being a significant component of the Atlanteans diet. This had significant effects on their intellect and memory retention.

A portion of their water was processed through crystals at a nearby lake, ensuring that the water contributed to nurturing and balancing people's energetic fields at the same time. Fish caught from the sea were accepted graciously, and too much was never taken, only enough for that day, ensuring that the freshness of the fish ably nourished the people of Atlantis.

Fish from the sea then were pure and free of mercury. There was no plastic for any sea creature to battle or accidentally consume, and no place under the ocean where rubbish fell and melded with the earth.

The Atlanteans had a perfect balance of living with the sea and the earth, and this was reflected in their everyday life in every way. Both were worshipped for their contribution, and respect was given to them daily.

What we miss now from the earth is the sense of all living together as one.

Where once we lived knowing that if other creatures die, we also die, now we assume that human beings will rise above all things.

We do not respect the interconnectedness of all things and that if something is taken away, all things are, including life, which brings us to the next universal law, the web of life.

LAW 9: THE WEB OF LIFE

When one creature falls, it is the beginning of a global fall. When the life of one plant or animal species is lost, this impacts the whole.

There is no way of avoiding the impact that this loss will make; we can merely try to learn from our mistakes and ensure it does not happen again.

There are certain species such as bees, birds, and other wildlife crucial to our survival as they propagate the plant life that we feed from. Without these vital few, the connectedness between plant and animal life breaks down, and we will see further famine and loss.

When we do not respect the connection of everything to each other, we fail to see how fragile human life on earth is. If we could be shown this in a way and timeline we could understand, without arrogance clouding our vision, we would see the difference between human life existing or not existing is only ten years.

There are some animals you are aware of that are important, such as bees. However, there are some you are not, and it is not our job to tell you what these species are as it is your role as caretakers of the earth to preserve the whole, not just those that serve human beings' needs.

It is in the most unlikely of places you will find the plants and animals who hold the keys to life on earth. And it is in the most unlikely of places you will not look for answers when the world begins to fall.

In the web of life and the law of it, it is not our role to play god and choose who lives and dies.

It is our role to protect all living creatures, plants, and everything that has consciousness. Therefore, do not look at the bees and think about how you can save them. Instead, look at everything around you and how you can preserve it in all its glory and beauty.

The only way we can change the world and respect the web of life is by respecting the area we live in and consume from.

If you can see life in all things around you, you will be living by the law of the web of life. If you kill or maim anything that lies within your realm or others, you are not respecting the web of life. To kill another being, for-profit or protein is to take from yourself, your existence, and your soul.

While we understand that life on earth must be enjoyable and we must survive as all creatures do, we must respect the web of life and only take what we need from it. To take more than what we need is to enact the law of the web of life, and its consequences are severe.

Remember that everything around you is living and you'll do well in this world. Preserve and help other things to grow, and you will live a good and healthy life here. Tune into yourself, look after your backyard, and you will see the change you wish to see in the world.

32

KNOWING

When our actions do not match our words, we cause an imbalance in the universe and the world around us. When we do not listen to the words being spoken to us and act on them, we are causing an imbalance in the world around us.

In today's world, so many great words spoken, but the world chooses not to listen as we continue to choose comfort over discomfort and certainty over uncertainty. It is almost certainly easier to know and come to grips with the fact that the world is going to end rather than doing something about it.

Who knows what to do when the problem is so large? Who knows what to do when the very problem that exists comes back to the core of our beings?

In each chapter on earth, one species comes into control or dominance eventually. It always begins in balanced and always ends as imbalanced. When we do not listen and let our need for instant gratification take hold, we lose in every way.

When we do not take advantage of the time we are given to 'do something,' we lose too because we forget what it is like to win when we always play what feels like a losing game.

And how does a group of people who do not care about power, money, or politics rise against the most influential forces in the world, power, money, and politics?

It may feel like a losing game, but it does not need to be. It may feel like we can never catch up, but we can. And it may feel like this was always destined to end, but we should not resign ourselves to this.

The next few years are about re-birth on earth, but we must do this the right way, and we need your help.

33

EXCESS

The deterioration of the earth, its produce, plants, and animals will not be slow.

The re-establishment of the right powers on earth will be swift, with humanity being brought to its knees in a way it cannot remember.

Humans were merely a species in control of the earth for a short period of time, a group of people who used violence to get what they needed to survive and killed anything in their path that blocked them from achieving it.

So much of life on earth is about death and destruction. So much is about power and taking power from others to strengthen the state, the government, and the people.

What we must realize is that it was never about 'taking' as there was always enough. When the earth began, there was always enough if one group did not take more than they needed. This was a lesson, and human beings have failed miserably at it.

Some may argue this is not true as look at how much famine there is in the third world. However, if you look back to the dawn of time and to the times of Atlantis, you will now understand there was always more than enough.

Excess and abundance is only something we have come to know in modern times because luxury is craved, and to have more than enough is perceived to be the only way to live. If there are so many people living with tremendous wastage, wouldn't this food, water, and clothing best go to other people who do not have even enough fresh water to drink?

Earth has become a cruel place, and despite so many people having so much, more human beings than ever feel dead inside. Lifeless, dull, and surrounded by more expensive items than they could ever want or appreciate.

The reason we are sharing the story of Atlantis is that there is a recipe for happiness and balance, and we can get back to this, but first, we must lose the mindset we have about wealth, the power of comparison, and how we see ourselves.

Success is not a nice car, house, and land package. It is looking after ourselves, our family, community, and the greater world around us. It is only through giving back that we will receive and feel full, which brings us to the law of illusions.

34

LAW 10: ILLUSIONS

The law of illusions is when we take more than what we need, and no matter how beautiful or wonderful the item is, it makes us feel empty. This is why the more we have, the emptier our hearts, minds, and souls can become.

When we have enough, and we take no more than this, our spectrum of happiness and heartfulness is unlimited in its capacity because we do not look to the world for 'things,' we look to it for life.

Atlantis and the people who lived within it were in a perfect state of balance when Kelipah arrived. It was when Kelipah showed them a world of excess for the first time they questioned if this excess could make them even happier?

It could not, but they needed to learn this for themselves.

What Kelipah offered them seemed simple. A gold vase for some information. A casket made of gold to stay overnight. Simple exchanges and trades. This was until the ultimate vow was broken and became not a few items in excess, but a life of excess if the people of Atlantis gave their souls to Kelipah. But they did not know it was their souls in jeopardy; they only knew it meant more beautiful items in their houses.

One could argue that if people can attain more, then what is the problem? The challenge is that human beings have an insatiable nature for more.

The law of illusion teaches us that once we reach a certain point of status, wealth, and bureaucracy, we cannot find any more joy in what we buy, own, or find, which is what we must learn.

The journey to happiness begins within and will never be found in the objects we collect or seek. Where a life of excess to those who are poor looks indulgent and carefree, the weight it bears on those who are rich is just as heavy as the emptiness of someone poor on their toughest days. Life's lessons do not evade us in our wealth or lack of it.

Living in castles painted with gold does not make you a master; it makes you a slave. And when you work as a slave hoping to become a master, you have begun a race that is relentless and never ends.

If you realize you do not need either, you will bypass the law of illusion and see the truth: that we were brought here to learn and evolve our inner being, not our outer one.

When we can see all of the illusions around us, we can free ourselves from them.

CURRENCY

Kelipah was not a bad man, just as we are not all bad.

Human beings have merely become accustomed to taking what we want or feel we need, and Kelipah was no different.

Atlantis was one of the greatest, yet most unknown cities in the world in his time. He had heard of their excess, but excess was not a concept here. It was merely they were in perfect equilibrium with nature, plants, animals, crystals, and the elements. And it was this relationship of working together that created its beauty.

They adored the sea, and the sea adored them and always brought what they needed. The air and wind adored them, therefore always brought air that was fresh and what was needed in wind that day. A great deal of the city was powered by wind, and every few days, the element of air would come to top up their power.

The earth was always fertile and grew the most beautiful

crops because the people of Atlantis were kind to the earth. And fire was a worthy and much-loved companion of Atlantis and lit the city's pathways just as the crystals did in the mornings and evenings as people made their way about their daily business.

Everything in Atlantis was a relationship of love and perfect synergy. There was respect for each other, and every species and creature had its place in the web of life. There was a thirst for knowledge, but it was to learn more about the world and our environment, not to use this knowledge to create new products and grow their riches.

Currency did not exist in Atlantis because it did not need to as everything was paid for in love and respect.

Money can be a tool for positive change or a reminder of who is valuable and who is not according to modern society. It is assumed if you have money, you must be valuable. If you do not, you must not. This is a simplistic and unfair way to rule the world when every human being has beautiful and important gifts to share.

When you measure yourself based on your wealth or how well you are doing working within a system that never intended to be fair, you will never be happy.

What is hard about the earth currently is that we are all learning many lessons concurrently. Some are paying for the lessons of others, and some are still learning these lessons ourselves. The more we can learn to value ourselves and not the riches we keep in our houses and the money, or lack of it, in our pockets, the more we can be free.

To aspire to money is to aspire to be within a system that will not last. When the world's currency fails, and technology shuts down, leaving us with nothing more than plastic cards, it will not be money that will save us. It will be ourselves.

When our pockets are empty, and we no longer have money to earn or buy products or services, it will be how much we have learned about the world that will allow us to survive.

When we buy everything we need from a store and not realize that the greatest store ever created on earth was mother earth herself, we have already lost the battle but not the war.

When we win the war, it will be against ourselves, not against an imaginary invader, enemy, an economy or against an invisible scale of what it means to be valuable in today's society.

When we learn to value ourselves and know that nothing we ever own could ever measure our value, we will be free. And when we learn we were only ever here to be ourselves and no-one else, we will have accomplished the greatest feat on earth: to know the power of thyself and nothing else.

36

INFORMATION

Atlantis was a peaceful nation with no weapons or wars.

No-one carried knives or needed self-protection as none were familiar with the art of war or combat. To try and take a city requires a battle, but how would Kelipah battle with a place that does not know the concept of it?

He could not, and this is why he fought for information as information could bring down the city. But first, he needed to create a currency of sorts, and that currency would be lies.

When those in Atlantis began accepting gifts from Kelipah, they realized they had done the wrong thing, yet they could not help themselves. And when Kelipah brought them even more gifts, all they could do was accept and close the doors of their houses so that others could not see the wealth they were accumulating.

What you must understand is that in Atlantis, the doors were never closed to houses. Because the weather was so beautiful, warm and balmy, there was never any need. Theft was something that didn't exist, and people respected others enough to value their privacy. Therefore, why close doors when you do not need to keep anything in?

It was when doors began to close in Atlantis that a corrupt currency had been created. It was when people started noticing the closing of doors that Kelipah's eyes lit up with glee. He now had information that could be bought and sold, and others were coming to him for this information. Who had what and where? Who had been given what, and what else did they ask for?

In only days, greed had become the newest resident of Atlantis, and what this gave Kelipah was tremendous power. Despite having a ship filled with many great and powerful weapons, he did not need to use them.

What Atlantis had unearthed in itself was that information was more powerful than anything else on earth. And it would be information that would bring down the city and place Kelipah in a chair that had never existed before, as president of Atlantis. A place he did not deserve, nor did he come looking for. Kelipah was not a leader; he was a warrior and businessman.

What Atlantis needed was a way out, but they could not provide themselves that when all their hearts craved was more, and Kelipah said he could give it to them.

When Kelipah realized he could use the information he had

over others to elevate himself into the highest position of power, it was only a matter of time until Atlantis sunk beneath the waves.

Using information, Kelipah had created a currency more valuable than gold, and this is the same situation we are in today.

None of what you see is real. It has all been used as currency to move somewhere higher. Yes, money is still involved, but what we must all realize and see in the world is that information, our personal information, and what the world has over all of us is more powerful than anything else on earth. And while we may use this information to better our lives, we also worsen them by being part of a game that was never destined to be played.

LOVING SPIRITS

What we must do on earth is crystallize the vision of the world we wish to create, not the one that exists now or to repair what we already have. We must work to create the planet and the earth we wish to live in.

If we had an opportunity as human beings to create a loving, safe, and warm place, free from harm, what would we create?

Would there be walls to keep certain groups in? Would there be a place to escape to if there was war?

No, there would not because the world we need to build is one where creativity and equality reigns. A world where we can be ourselves without fear of being harmed for being the humans, souls, and spirits we were born to be.

In Atlantis, creativity and individuality were celebrated. No-one was cut down for being smarter, more creative, or beautiful than somebody else. The people of Atlantis loved and cherished the uniqueness of the people, plants, and animals around them and knew that for the earth to be sustained and to flourish, we would need people, plants, and animals from all walks of life.

Atlantis recognized that people are born of love, and love is our nature, but it must also be nurtured.

We can be born as loving spirits and souls, but if we are not shown love, this part of us, like a tree without water, shrivels and dies. This is how happiness and sadness is created on earth. Those who are happy are shown love, and those who are unhappy are left to wither away and die.

All people, plants, animals, and elements deserve love, affection, and respect. How different would the world and universe be if we had all of these three things from birth? How many fewer wars would there be if we were cherished for our strengths and weaknesses?

Our Achilles heel must be loved as much as the strength of our bow and the straightness of our arrow. How well we hit the target of what we are here to achieve on earth is how loving our teacher is when we are taught to shoot forth our destiny.

If we are brave, we will love all others as we love our family and friends. We would treat all others the same and show them the love we would expect to be shown ourselves, but we must have good teachers who show us love in a way that is not conditional, but unconditional.

To find love, we must look for it in the right, not the wrong places. To go to someone for love who has not been taught the real qualities of love is to come up empty or short.

To ask for love to fill us up and heal us is not love either as we must fill up the love within ourselves, and if we have a good and wise teacher, we are able to do this.

The less we can look to others for love and find it in ourselves, the happier we will be. The less we can look to others for direction, the happier and more fulfilled we will feel. And finally, the less we can look to another to step into our soul to fill us, this is where we will find fulfillment, purpose, solidarity, and truth from our fellow humankind.

To show ourselves under the moonlight, the sunlight, and at dawn, when the day is coldest and just beginning, is when we know we are our true selves all of the time. When the one who ventures into the night is different from the one who ventures into the day shows us, there may be many masters of the one soul.

We must seek to integrate and disintegrate the parts of ourselves that stop and hinder the progress of the soul. We must seek to support the true self stepping forward even when this brings us into a state of fear and discomfort. And what we must realize is that by being ourselves, we permit the world to be itself too.

To show ourselves love and total compassion, in moments of strength and weakness, is to begin the journey we call life.

We love you and cherish you for who you are, who you will be, and everything in between. But right now, we need your help to restore the earth to its former glory and balance. Each of you has a role, and this is what you must seek to find out.

The reason Atlantis worked so well is each Atlantean knew they would be born into a role that would make the most of their strengths, weaknesses, and character flaws.

When we embrace ourselves fully and completely, we are never lost, we are only on the way to being found.

# IGNORANCE

As the tides rose, the Atlanteans had two choices, raise the walls and platforms the city was built on or repair their relationship with the water. They did neither.

As peaceful beings, the Atlanteans had no comprehension of the damage that had been done. No war had broken out, the city was not in a famine, although there were some now going with less food than before and others with more. And there was no way of knowing how the elements would rise to reclaim what was theirs: this palace that lay on the sea.

When we do not understand what we have, we cannot know what we are going to lose.

The challenge with the mindset of the people of Atlantis is they took for granted their relationships with the elements would remain the same. Yet they did not notice that the respect they had for each element grew a little less each day with the arrival of Kelipah and his men in the city.

They did not realize that when you do not pay homage to the water daily and respect her greatness and power that she may choose not to keep her waves at bay. But this is too simple of a way at looking at what happened in Atlantis as several different factors caused its downfall.

Part of it is to do with the web of life, but part of it is due to ignorance.

What we do not understand as a human species on earth is we are each responsible for a part of the earth and its inhabitants. We are each born to look after or do one thing that upholds and keeps the balance of the earth and the people, plants, and animals that live upon it.

When we go to work every day to earn money, and we do not think of the earth, something is missing. When we go to work, and we think about helping save the earth, but if it does not go any further than thought, something is missing.

The people of Atlantis each found their purpose; however, each began to slowly forget their relationship and the commitment they had made to the earth, instead pledging their love and allegiance to inanimate objects and wealth. Neither of these will help the earth become more in balance. Both tip us further out of balance, and this is what we must realize.

If each of us knows we are important, then each of us knows what we all do over the next two to three years is crucial to our survival.

If globally, we can all see and realize what our potential is and not just think about it, but do it, we have a chance at saving our home and hearts of those we love.

This is not a choice, as the re-balancing of the earth will happen anyway. What we must establish is how much we can resolve as a species and how much of our lives and livelihoods will be taken away when the re-balancing occurs.

ANCIENT PEOPLE

When we cannot establish what we must do next, we cannot know how to undo all that we have done.

If we listen to scientists and not politicians, we will know what to concern ourselves with.

Politicians work for money, and scientists work for answers. When looking for answers, we must look to what the industry is saying as a whole, particularly in the areas of global warming and climate change.

Our leaders will not want to invoke fear and panic within us as their interest is control. It is our scientific leaders we should look to in this time of change for the answers we're seeking.

If we look to conservationists and key projects around the world, we will see which parts of the earth are being obliterated fastest for increased money and power. It is these projects we must stand with and the governments and businesses we must stand against to take these parts of the world back and restore ownership to the natural inhabitants of the land.

It is these ancient people who know how to look after the lands they were born into, not business or the economy that should be dictating how this land is used or consumed. In reality, it should never be consumed as it is the home for so many animals, plants, human beings, and insects.

When we slay the rainforests, we forget how many homes we are destroying for the menial things we love and could go without. We must ask why and stand with the trees before they are all destroyed. Where will we be without oxygen? And where will we be without our faith in humanity when we have lost faith in ourselves?

What we must realize and remember is that life was never destined to be this way. Life and living were never destined to be about consumption or destroying things for pleasure. We were never destined to hunt animals or humans for our enjoyment, as this goes against the nature of who we are and the web of life.

Everything in our existence, apart from inanimate objects of human creation, is a living and wonderful thing, despite how small or insignificant it may feel or seem to be. Even the worms of our earth carry a particular purpose in digging up and mulching the soil, so it is fertile for our crops. Every ant is consuming something that needs to be consumed or taking something somewhere for a purpose or reason. We do not need to understand what the reasons are, but we must give them respect for the journey they have taken to reach this place and allow them to complete the work they are destined to do even if their life seems short compared to ours.

When we take the life of another, even something as small in size as an ant, we are cutting the life of something else short, which has an impact on the earth.

Yes, we must live, and to live, we must either consume plants, animals, wheat or grasses, but we must never take the life of something else out of pleasure or disdain for its existence. Many ants, spiders, moths, and caterpillars have disdain for our existence as we create many products that are purely for their destruction, yet they do not rise as a species to kill or consume us.

Spiders have this power and the volume and strength in numbers to do this, but they do not see the point in trying to destroy another creature. They merely eat what they need to and move on, which is the difference between us and other creatures who inhabit the earth. Where we see something or someone and dislike them for how they have been made, other creatures do not.

Where we will kill our own kind to create a 'master race' or bomb entire cities to punish others for the deeds they have done, animals nor plants do not.

We are a species all of our own, and where we were initially born loving, we have moved so far from this path. We are not who we were born to be, and this sadness and disconnect should have the ability to strike all of us down in our tracks. Yet it does not, and we continue to harm and maim all of those around us.

We have missed the point of respect long ago, and we must work to gain the respect of the animals, plants, and elementals around us.

If we can bring the earth back into balance and ourselves back into love, we have a chance at regaining all we have lost. Although, all is not possible as so many beautiful species have been taken by our bullets and bellies as we fight for power in a war that does not exist.

40

SECRETS

Information is the most priceless asset on earth. It goes above art as art can be corrupted and copied. It goes above money as more of it can simply be made, and it goes above love as love can be broken down with information.

What Kelipah had over every person in the city was a series of spies and eyes who would gather and collect information for him from across the city. Kelipah's men would bring him the findings of the day, and Kelipah would write all of this under each family name written in a large, black leather-bound book which he kept in his office.

Kelipah's office began as merely a table in his room at the Inn and ended up being the most powerful room in Atlantis, the oracle room, and this is where Kelipah kept his ever-growing book.

Kelipah's goal was to bring the city to its knees, and he did this by letting others know that he had a special book with notes written on the comings and goings of each family.

What is interesting is that each family began as pure and was merely going about life as they always had, but the invention of this book made them more secretive, and when secrets arise, this is when we can be bought and sold like cattle.

This is what is happening today with our inside versus outside personas, and what we do not realize this book has already been created. The governments are simply waiting to use it when the time is right. There is much collusion in the world today, and it goes between both brands and governments, secret organizations, and those run in the public eye.

What we see is never the whole picture, and we will never see it, even when the world around us and its traditional structures come tumbling down.

When we look at ourselves now, we are just like the people of Atlantis, but we are far further down the track with the cruelty we commit and the secrets we keep.

The next few years will travel quickly, and the rebalance will be swift. Will you be ready?

… 41

SLOW

The tides are changing, but we do not watch the tides enough to see where they are going.

Over the next two years, we will see tremendous changes on earth in our lives, atmosphere, and the air we breathe.

If we are aware, we will see that while many will choose to stay and live in the cities, many will feel a calling to move to the country and get away. Many will feel the need for a sea change over the coming years, but many will not know why.

What it is, is a biological need for survival. What we must re-learn to do is support ourselves and our families without the pleasures of the big city. What we must embrace is the lesson of slowness and adapting to life at the pace in which it should have been lived, originally, and thoughtfully.

What we must realize is that there are other ways of living life, and these other ways should be embraced as they are more enjoyable, sustainable, and nourishing than how we are living now. Those who move to the country will realize this, but even then, we still rely on our crops to be provided in packages produced in the big city or in commercial facilities across the country or world.

What we ask you to do is look at life and how you can live more naturally and in sync with the earth.

How can you learn to love her and live with her? How can you ask her to help you make this adjustment? How can you ask her to show you how to live in a new way, creating a new life for you, your family and your friends? There is a way, and she can show you, but you must be open to these changes, and with these changes, you must change yourself.

When you can embrace 'slow' and slowness, you can learn to live in conjunction with the seasons, what they produce, and how you can re-nourish the earth so that she can keep providing for you. This is all we ask of you, to respect her, to help save her, and to nourish her as she has nourished you your whole life and never asked for anything in return.

Earth is on her knees now, malnourished and under cared for. Will you help her return to her former glory? Will you help her rise against a humanity that is killing her for their survival, never realizing for a second that without her, we are nothing. We are only here for a moment and a second in the scheme of time itself, how will you make your time worthwhile? How will you help set earth free from the commercial chains that bind her?

42

SUPER WAVES

If you've ever looked at the face of a wave, you will have been awed by its beauty, the curve of its lip, and the way you can see through it to see what lies within.

There is a moment of gracefulness as the tower of it rises and a sense of inevitability that this beauty will topple.

We love to admire the beauty of waves, but in their rawest element, they are nature's show of power. Just as the wind in a hurricane is a show of power, so are the waves on any beach on any given day.

What waves do when they reach a higher level of power with more volume behind them is not create more waves, instead, they make taller waves. It is like the wave itself summons the power of the ocean and calls to bring more force and thunder to its already powerful existence. It is when enough volume is collected that we see super waves, tidal waves, or tsunami's as human beings call them.

UNIVERSAL LAW

The image of a tidal wave is almost too large for the mind of a human being to understand, as being so close to such a beast inevitably means death.

We believe these moments of power come by chance, but they do not. They are all chosen, although the death that occurs is not. Some humans may say its a case of wrong place, wrong time, whereas others would say 'God' is punishing the earth.

It is not punishment, it is a rebalance, and this is what is coming for us on earth. A series of rebalances called natural disasters to bring humanity back into submission and right the wrongs occurring on earth.

What we carry on earth as human beings today are the crimes of our forefathers and our forebears who wronged the earth, and since then, no-one has been strong enough to correct our path. No-one has had the power to fight the tidal wave of corruption and self-gains in politics, business, and beyond, and this sea of money and what it has created rises topples down upon us.

We are the wave that has been building for thousands of years, and we are about to topple on and destroy everything innocently laying in our path.

We are the tidal wave, and while we fear what nature can bring, we should fear ourselves as we are the only ones who bring harm to our planet.

We are the threat, and there is no other way to look at ourselves other than in this way. On the inside, we want to be good, whole, and pure in our intentions, but we are driven by a world that already has its black book on us and all of our deeds.

The Atlanteans were a peaceful race, and we can become this way again if we disengage from the governments and the tentacles they wrap around us in faux care that creates real harm across the planet we have come to call home.

It is only when we realize this we will be able to be truly free again. It is only when we rise against the wave and know there is a chance to swim through it if we swim before it topples we can find strength in a new way. And it is only when we are strong enough to see through the wave and see it for what it truly is, power without mercy, that we will be re-born.

FIGHT

To know the wave, we must know what it is like to be inside it, and this is why we tell you the story of Kelipah.

Kelipah is every government and business around the world that works for consumption and the creation of more greed.

Kelipah is the parts of ourselves we find ugly but use to survive in this world. And Kelipah is the part that believes if we can just take one more thing, promotion or house, we will be free. We will never be free when we feel the need to take from others and the world around us.

It is only when we are comfortable with what we have and only having what we need we will reach a level of freedom that others do not have. It is only when we train our minds and our bodies to live without we will understand the plight of a nation that has gone through war or famine. And it is only when we can empathize with others and the world around us we will have it in our hearts to change.

Kelipah did not care about Atlantis even though he pretended to preserve its way of life. Kelipah saw Atlantis as an unreal place that did not fit with the rest of the world. So instead of keeping the world out of Atlantis, he brought the world and all its faux pleasures and pains in. He brought currency to a place that did not need it.

He brought taxes to a place that never required tax because no-one ever went without, and he brought secrecy to a land that had no secrets. Did the Atlanteans allow him to do this? Yes, but they did not know what they were letting in, just as human beings did not know what they were letting in when we saw the balance on earth shift.

If there was ever a time to fight for earth, its people, and those who are currently going without, it is now. Many people on earth are born and die again too quickly because the wealthier countries take more than what they need leaving poorer countries with the after-effects of a tidal wave they did not create. Yet we only notice the poorer countries when the crashes come and take life away.

We only know of Syria when the bombs are dropping, and we only know of Ethiopia when we see yet another child dying of starvation. Yet we fill our tv screens and minds with burgers, social media, and more jobs, money, toys, and more gifts for those around us.

What we do not realize is that the real gift is life, and to live freely just as an animal in the wild did before humanity corrupted the earth is what we must seek out.

We are the burden we have created for ourselves, and it is us that must unburden and unshackle ourselves from the life and livelihoods we have created. This is how we will be free, and it is when we escape to the mountains, free of the cities and concrete wastelands we have created that we can go back to living from the earth in a way that is respectful and kind.

We do not give you advanced warning or these lessons because we want humanity to die. We give you them because we want you to live in the way that was intended for you, not a fast track to a desolate corporate wasteland with no trees, plants or animal life.

No product could ever replace the life of an animal that has become extinct due to our need for more. Just as no earth is complete without all of its plants and animals, but it is too late for that.

44

MORE

Life is perceived to be better with the more we have, and it is only when our houses become full to the brim that we will buy bigger houses to store everything we own.

The plight of the human race is not that we do not have love in our hearts, because we do. The plight of the human race is that we do not and cannot realize when enough is enough.

At what point do we realize we have everything we need? This is the trap as with every new product, upgrade or update, we have a constant need for more. To catch up? Why? To not feel lost? We were lost long ago. To feel free? How can we be when the very things we believe are freeing us are trapping us?

If we were to live life only with nature and with what nature brought us, we would be free. If only we knew the joys that nature brings, we would feel happy in a way that no human-made product can make us. And we would feel free in a way that has not been seen on earth for many thousands of years.

We are a product of our own creation, and Atlantis is the most recent memory of when life was going to plan as we hoped it would, before Kelipah of course. Kelipah was our undoing, just as there are particular leaders in the world today that will be our undoing too. If only we could see what is beyond the next wave? If only we could see what is coming?

Of course, we can, if you are willing to look and brave enough to see and believe what we are telling you in this book. We do not share these laws and these histories for our benefit; we share it for yours, and it is for this reason that we share the universal law of profit.

LAW 11: PROFIT

When we take from the earth, and we do not repay it for its gifts, there is a tax placed on our heads and our hearts.

This tax comes in a nondescript form, such as unplanned life events and temporary setbacks. Some of us are still paying these debts today from many lifetimes ago. However, we can free ourselves from this if we serve the earth and only her.

If we work for the earth in our 'jobs,' but we spend our money on propelling useless consumption in the world, we will find more tax added to our debts. If we can work with a kind and happy heart, in service and respect of the earth, living by the rules and practices we preach, we can avoid such debts and minimize what we owe.

If we have a business that is practicing sustainability and equality on the outside, but on the inside undermines people, paying them a lesser price for the work they do and the business profits for their excellent image, the debt incurred will be higher.

If, however, a business practices sustainability, equality, environmental consciousness, and employees are treated with love, care, and respect, the tax you will pay to profit will be far less if not non-existent.

What we see today are many businesses that are not congruent with their mission statements and their practices. What we see are many faces wearing many masks playing a role to increase their profits, never realizing the debts they are accruing in universal law.

The debts we pay in human currency are far less than the debts we must pay the universe if we help tip her even further out of balance.

If you are the owner of a business not congruent with the original intent for your business and its sustainability practices, your debt on earth will rise.

While you may hide the figures in your books, you cannot hide what you are making and taking from the earth. Only we know this, and this is a debt you will settle with us, which may take many lifetimes depending on how much you have profited and not given back.

The universal law of profit must be obeyed if we are to continue to survive here on earth. We cannot continue to take without giving back, as this is the equivalent of theft in the eyes of universal law.

Yet if we take and then give back, live sustainably, and with love in our hearts, we can lessen the debt and help create an earth fruitful for future generations.

When corruption and theft on earth cease, we will find a new way to exist, and on this day, the sun will shine brighter than ever.

PREPARATION

How we see the world impacts how we work and play within it.

When we see the world as our farm and place to reap all of the goodness that nature has created, we do not have the right vision. When we see the world as a place we are privileged to live in and know our place within it, we have a healthier perception.

At no time since Atlantis has there been complete peace and harmony in one place. Atlantis is the last known example of this in the memory and stories of human beings.

Atlantis is the last known example of human beings living with the earth and everything in its creation in harmony.

There have been times where we have forgotten the distance between us and others, moments of freedom in a world of slaves. Still, Atlantis is the example we hold above all else because it was the best example of everything moving in perfect synchronicity and harmony.

The world we intend to build will be built on the principles of Universal Law, and there are those building these cities around the world right now. Everything is already in progress. There are certain places and hubs we have recognized as ideal places to be rebuilt, and these are the locations you must seek out. They do not lie in the cities, nor do they lie too close to the water. On higher ground, away from the main thoroughfare and out of harm's way.

If you ask to find these places and you are living in the right way, respectfully and equally with your peers, plants, and animals, these places will be shown to you perhaps in dreams, visions, or someone will speak directly to you about them.

We are preparing for an age of enlightenment again, but we have a way to go before we are ready for this. Much like a play, there will be an intermission period where one act closes, as another prepares to open. It is at this moment we will need these burgeoning cities the most as we prepare for what's to come and deal with the downfall of what has been.

One day the cities we call home now may be in dusty deserts or have been consumed by the waves and sit as ancient relics underwater, intact, covered in the ocean's grime.

The time it takes to build cities like Atlantis is what is imperative right now. The time it will take to prepare us, the mental strength we will need to survive this new era, as this act closes, and we still proudly believe we are a super race.

There is no super race without water, air, fire, or earth. This is logic, and any smart man, woman, or child on earth can see this. To think we can continue to rise above everything when half the world is starving is an arrogant thought in a world desperately in need of more empathy.

In the scheme of history and time on earth itself, Atlantis did not take a long time to build. It was the thought that went into it that made it one of the smartest cities in the world. It was the relationship the people of Atlantis had with nature and the world around them that allowed the elements to help, not hinder the journey of this great city.

Atlantis was not built in a day or a year, but what it did create in our history was an example of when the world worked together for the greater good of all.

47

ADAPT

Adopting the ways of others can work to our benefit or detriment.

The lives we lead are incredibly complex. We read self-help books to get ahead, and we are continually changing and adapting our routines to fit a world we cannot keep up with.

If the world is a high-speed train, we lost control of the accelerator and the brake a long time ago. What we have instead is a train on a collision course with the end of the tracks. There is no circling back, nor is there another route we can take. We have always been heading in this direction; it is just that the people of this time will experience both the end and a new beginning. This is why you are all here, and each of you has a part to play.

To be on earth at this time is a great privilege, but it will also not be easy.

In our lives and hearts, we naturally hope for the best and

assume that 'it'll never happen to us.' In our lifetime, it will be us watching the world fall around us. It will be us watching natural disasters strike the earth as landmarks we have come to love and admire fall at our feet. It will be us left questioning 'Why has this happened?', when the better question to ask is 'Why did we not listen?'.

Why did we not listen when the warning signs were there? Why did we not listen when we were told that the earth's core and the atmosphere was heating up? And why did we not teach our children about the earth and how to protect her?

If we wish to continue living on earth, we must look after her in a way we have never thought to before. We must cherish the wind and everything she brings, just as we cherish the sky, moon, stars, and the sun.

We must not waste water as one day she will be more difficult to find. We must cherish fire for the warmth it brings and be grateful it helps keep disease at bay, allowing us to heat our food and warm our bodies.

Human beings in the future will live with a lot less than we do now. There are those who see the world as it is now, speaking quietly among themselves about what's to come, but no-one is talking loudly enough about what will eventually consume us.

The chrysalis of time is that time does not exist, nor should it need to. We are giving you warning so you have time to learn what you need to before the re-balancing occurs.

What you learn at this time is up to you. What you take from us and what you are prepared to absorb and process is up to you. This is not a game; it is a partnership between us all. The agreement we have always had with the inhabitants of earth is that if you were prepared to care for this great planet, we would allow you to live here as long as you needed to. This agreement has stretched, and we have been patient.

Like parents with teenagers, we have accepted your untidiness, moods, and your wrath when life has not gone to plan. We have loved you when you have sat in your room, hating us, and we have given you strength when you told us to leave. We are the ever-watchful, patient spirits that observe you from afar and offer you all the love in the world if you are willing to take it, but you do not, and you have not. It is this relationship we are seeking to rectify before it is too late.

We are the hand extended waiting for you to hold it, and when you do, you will notice everything in your life will be re-balanced and restored. Life is not always what we plan, but where would the fun and mystery be in living if we knew how the cards were dealt ahead of time?

THOUGHTFULNESS

To chart a course in history that is worthy of being chartered, we must look at everywhere we have been before and know that none of these ways were the right ways.

We do not look at history enough and what it has tried to teach us. We do not take stock of lessons of the past and how easily we fell into them with the wrong leadership and a fearful way of thinking.

For us to take back the earth, we must be fearless. Death is coming for us anyway; we must fight for our future generations and what they will inherit. We have already caused so much pain by our need for more when we could have taken less.

We have caused so much struggle when our need to rise means crushes others to reach the top. If we are to change our ways, first we must change our world and how we see ourselves and our place within it.

The lives we lead in this time do matter, and the time-sensitive nature of what we are trying to achieve could not be more pressing than it is now. If we do not change our minds and ways, we will find the world we once loved lost to the ashes.

The sunrises and sunsets were more beautiful in Atlantis than today because there was no light or chemical pollution. The sky was pure, just like the air. The water was fresh, crystal clear, and not one chemical existed at this time. Oils came from olives, but not oil spills.

Plants were able to grow without pots or pruning. Everything was wild and in its most beautiful, natural form and this is why we thrived because we were wild too. Not in the way you would think now, which is wild hair and ways, but wild in the sense that we were free and not enslaved to technology, machines, or false deadlines.

There were no jobs as we each contributed with the gifts we had, which meant full minds and hearts. We saw each other as spirits living within a divine physical body. We saw ourselves as free, and because we were free, the idea of slavery never existed.

We each fell in love, and love did not mean entrapment or beatings. There was no jealousy as no-one went without. There was no fame because no-one needed to be famous. The world was equal, and each person, plant, and animal shone without the need to outshine another. If we could go back to this time, we would, but this would mean a long journey home, and we are not asking for this yet as we will need to progress to proceed to this place with a calm head and calm heart.

What we are asking is that you simply ask 'What if?' and then begin working towards creating an equal planet. Do not ask 'What will I take today? but instead 'What won't I take today?'. We must begin to recognize the difference between needing and wanting, taking and receiving, giving thanks, and paying in currency without thought.

Thoughtfulness is all we ask for and all we wish to receive. It is a simple ask in a complicated world, but one that is achievable if we try.

Rest your mind and rest your heart, but not for too long as the fight to save ourselves and our planet will begin soon. Let the waters be calm in your heart, but not too calm that you withdraw for too long. And let your mind be free of the worries of what will come, and instead focus on positive and thoughtful action. We do not need big acts of sacrifice; we need small acts across the planet from all people.

SHIVA

When Atlantis fell, those around Atlantis lost their fear that something so catastrophic could ever happen again.

When they lost hope, those who had the intelligence to recognize what Atlantis was would weep for a city they had not known but had dreamt of every night as they slept.

And when they had lost their fear, it was not because they did not believe it would happen again, but because all people believe that when something terrible happens it buys us more time between events. There is a thought of 'if the gods have wreaked their pain and havoc it won't be wreaked again for some time as we have satisfied them'.

It was not us that caused the downfall of Atlantis, but it was us that needed to rebalance it as caretakers of the universe.

When Shiva and the elements came to rebalance the space, it was a swift execution but one that was always coming.

Some would think that this story is not positive and full of death and destruction. While this is true in many ways, how many years must we hide what happened in Atlantis while you think about her beauty? How long must we ignore her pain when it is so similar to our own?

Over the coming years, you must prepare for what is occurring and speak out and act against the violence you see in your world.

Too much in your world is already lost to waves, but the waves are not us even though it will be us that delivers the final blow. The waves are your greed and your lust for more in a world where so many already go without.

The trials and tribulations you must go through will not go to waste as they will help you learn what you do not want to create in the next chapter of your lives here on earth. Your history will help you know and understand all the ways not to run a city, a country, or the world.

The leaders in power are showing you how absurd the world has become and you must remember that you allowed them to be elected. While you can say vote or no vote you did not have a choice, you have always had choices. We have always had choices.

We choose how we act, how we see, what we hear, and what we do about what is directly in front of us. This is what you must remember. And do not just speak, act. Words are powerful yes, but followed with actions they are explosive.

50

SCHOLARS

On the most beautiful days in Atlantis, life was good.

The air was clear, and the sun was bright and warm. Love and light was found around every corner, and each place in Atlantis had its place under the sun. Light shone on all those who shone their light on the world, and in Atlantis, this was everybody.

Each person had a trade, service, or gift they offered, and each also worked in service of the planet and restoring her in every way they could.

In Atlantis, they understood the rest of the world was not in the same place as they were mentally, spiritually, and emotionally, hence why the Atlanteans did what they could to share resources and information with the books they created and shared with the world. They also invited scholars to come and share in the glory and create in this amazing space.

Mighty scholars, artists, and musicians they attracted in droves, and when these gifted people entered Atlantis, a light went on in themselves they had never seen before. The light was potential, and this was a gift, and light never went out.

In Atlantis, they saw the future of the world in a way they had never contemplated or imagined. They saw people, plants, animals, and all of earth's elements living in perfect harmony. They saw all people, no matter what their origin or wealth, treated with respect.

Each man, woman, and child was as high as another, and he or she was as equal as the crystal they stood next to or the ocean they stood upon. There was a sense of synchronicity, playfulness, but also deep respect and understanding of their place within the universe.

What Atlantis offered visitors to their city was time to create and explore their minds so that when they re-emerged back into the world, they would take a piece of Atlantis with them.

They would visit Atlantis only once unless they were invited to return, but those who did wish to come back would undertake a treacherous journey as the sea naturally guided people away from Atlantis and not to it.

To most people, Atlantis was a mirage that may or may not have existed. The lure and promise of the city were too great to dismiss, but to try and travel there would surely end in death, which was true for most, except Kelipah.

51

EMERALD

Think about how beautiful a city would be if it were built on the water surrounded by nature and made in crystals?

Imagine if you can all species living in harmony, with no human being, plant, or animal ever going without. How would the energy be? What would it feel like, and how would the city respond when it was given love?

This is an intriguing idea because if everything is alive and everything has a consciousness, then when everything is loved, it must respond with love. Think of the cities you visit today and how empty they feel, made of concrete with no natural materials in sight.

If you showed a city like New York love, it could not respond in return. The soul of the city was lost in its skyscrapers a long time ago. Whereas if a city is built from natural materials and not to excess, then if you send love from your heart to the heart of the city, it would respond with love. This is what Atlantis did.

Much like Oz's Emerald City was perceived to be a great and wonderful city, so was Atlantis as it was created with live materials.

When we think of the cities we build on and live in today; they are a place that houses many millions of people all living within a contained space with no nature or a token park to provide fresh air. Look at China and the air or lack of air they can breathe there.

We sacrifice so much of our quality of life for business and money, and if society falls, neither will matter. The only air you will care about and choose to breathe in is oxygen and not money, which you have come to depend on. The pieces of paper you love so much will be nothing when the world is on its knees, praying for salvation. This is what you must come to terms with and what you must plan for.

And when new cities arrive and rise as they will, as people across the world are working on this, these cities will be built from natural materials, and they will be shown love and love and protection will be shown in return. The cities will not be hollow as they are now, but sitting in nature, growing with it, full of life, and teeming with energy.

This is the world we wish to live in and what we will create again with the help of many hands and hearts.

KRISHNA'S PERSPECTIVE

On the day Atlantis fell, the breeze was calm and warm on my skin.

I felt the sun burn the back of my neck as I waited for what was coming. I do not speak of Atlantis from the perspective of an observer or a great lover of history. I was there, and this story is my story.

My role was to be a support and guide to the people of this place, but at no point was I to interfere with the lessons they were learning. So as Kelipah stepped to the forefront, I stepped back.

On the day life ended on Atlantis, I knew what was coming, and I prepared my body for the waves that would take it.

I sat with the elements and explained to them that they

should not fear me and take me as they would the others in Atlantis.

It was a sad day as just as I had watched this great civilization rise, I was about to watch it fall. I looked forward to going home as time on earth is never easy.

When the waves began to rise, and the water became higher than usual, I sat on the docks and watched as others went about their business, never noticing for a second what was coming. I sat and watched as the children played, and adults were consumed in their work and a new quest for riches. And I sat and watched; I could feel life slipping away, like a timer that was running out.

We do not fear death until it is upon us, but it is upon us far earlier than what we imagine. The moment we feel death is coming, death already holds us in its arms, waiting to take us away. Death comes for all of us and is not pleasant, but rebirth must occur. Rebirth is what Atlantis was experiencing, but not in the way we would hope it to be. It was the elements taking back what was theirs, and even for them, it was a sad but glorious day.

As I sat and watched the day unfold, and as the day turned to night, I stayed, and I waited for what was coming. There was no fear in me as I knew that fear was pointless. Life had ended for me many times before, and it would be no different on this day.

Life ended that day in Atlantis for all who lived there, and it ended for me too, which is why I can speak of it now.

LAW 12: REGENERATION

If we did not live in fear of death, when life slips away, it would not be scary. It would be the beginning of the next adventure, but we do not see death in this way.

On earth, we're taught life is about living, but life is about living as much as it is about death.

Death is what drives us to be stronger, fiercer, and to fight for what we wish to do here, and it is a powerful reminder time is running out. Death offers a chance to begin again, but only if it is by natural causes and when our time comes.

When karmic laws such as the law of regeneration come into effect, the only way to work with this law is to accept death as the beginning of something new and different.

The universal law of regeneration represents all that lives on earth and in the universe. Each element, particle, planet and all other living things will die eventually, some earlier or later than others.

We cannot escape death, which is why we must embrace it as a great and beautiful teacher of life. If we think of death most linearly, it is the place we all end up, and it is the period of time we are allowed to live for that defines how long it takes us to reach it.

On earth, we think of death as a terrible and finite thing. However, what death represents is the beginning of life, and this is what we do not see. I speak of this concerning when death comes for us at the time it was defined to come, not early or late.

When death comes for us too early because of the actions of others, disease, or unexplainable events, we lose the chance to do all that we came here to do. When death occurs at the right time, when we have done all we need to and completed the tasks our soul wishes to achieve, this is when we will experience our rebirth.

Death comes for us in one way or another, but it is the timing of it that defines the actions or results after.

If we are involved in taking the life of another, many karmic repercussions for this go on for many lives.

For us to regenerate, we must live and then die at the time the elements and earth wishes for our time to be over. It is at this point that the law of regeneration enables itself, and it is when this law is in effect that we can be reborn as a different being on this planet.

Death at the hand of another or ourselves does not guarantee this law to be effective as it is not abiding by the law. Other laws come into effect when a life is taken unnaturally, and this is what we must understand. Each soul must be at peace with the path they have traveled, but they must also be at peace with how long we ask you to travel the path for and what we wish you to achieve.

It is when you do and abide by this that you become strong. To leave this earth at the time of defined death and no sooner is to be reborn. To leave earlier is to wait for the justice the universe must hand down, based on how the death occurred. Death by your hand or by the hand of another requires resolution, but not in the way you think.

Karmic consequences do not happen instantly, nor do they occur in a way that could be seen as 'an eye for an eye.' That is a human way of thinking about death. Instead, we resolve these situations with the loving care of a mother or father trying to teach their child the ways of earth and the universe.

Death is an opportunity to be reborn, but it is also an opportunity to learn. Regeneration shows us that life can end in one way and be born in another. To travel this path is to be brave, to be bold, and to be free. To leave early sparks a new chain of events in the life of a soul.

We will care for those who have been taken too early. And we will punish those who took the life of another in a way that is balanced with the lives they have led and the pain they have enacted in each life. This is what you will not see, but know it exists and that we will always ensure life comes back into balance.

LAW 13: SURVIVAL

Carry yourself with the strength of an ox and the heart of a lion as the days to come are fraught with danger, and those you love may turn against you.

This is the universal law of survival.

When we go back to living from the earth without our houses, commercial products, supermarkets, grocery stores, and medical attention we are used to, the world will go wild for a time.

While there is 'peace' in lots of countries, more wars will erupt in this time than ever before, as those in power will aim to take any resources left on the planet and save them in stockpiles underground. You must be ready for this.

When the wars come, there will be famine, and you must have your own house built high in the mountains, away from the water and off the grid. You should not require anything from the people who previously served it to you in government.

None of the commercial providers will be up and running as their farms will be bombed, and their harvests will be empty. What you must learn to do is to grow your food and join a community where you can bring your skills to make this happen. There will be nothing worse than going hungry, yet we must all go hungry for a time to realize the damage we have done.

You will be safest high in the mountains away from the prying eyes of others and those who seek to do you harm. You will need to be strong enough and smart enough to protect your families, but you should not use missiles or guns.

You must work with the land and nature to protect what you have as they will work with you if your heart is true. And you must work with the people around you and find those who will share with you if you share with them.

What is complicated about the law of survival is that those who were generous in their hearts when they had money in the bank and food in their bellies may not be as generous in the fall. Just as those who had no money in the bank and little to no food now may be the most generous people you encounter because they are used to going without.

The journey we must all make over the coming years is realizing all that we do not need so we can decide on what we wish to create when the time comes to bunker down and hide.

If you can develop your relationship with the elements, the winters will go easier on you, just as the summers will not burn your skin. The less connected to the earth you are, the harder you will find the change. The more time you spend in nature, learning to love and understand her again, the easier you will find an open pathway into her heart when the time comes. She welcomes those who welcome and love her.

When times become tough and the nights cold, remember that she is the key to your survival and everything you need. And do not trust that the generosity you feel today will be there tomorrow when your family and friends are starving. We are built with the will to survive, but we are not taught how to survive, and this is what we must learn.

Some will try to steal from you, just as they have stolen from themselves over the years that have passed. Do not trust all who come your way as not all will have good intentions for you. Instead, judge each character as they enter the doors to your city, but do not judge their past actions. Instead, judge their heart and show them yours.

Go with your instinct and trust that all good people will find their way to you, but not all good people were good before just as not all good people who come to your door will still be good when the law of survival comes into effect.

We cannot trust that who we are today will be who we are

tomorrow. Survival brings out both the best and worst in us. Remember this, remember who you are today, know who you want to be tomorrow and who you want to be when the world falls.

Describe your intentions of who you wish to help. Describe your willingness to work with the earth and not against her. And lastly, wish for who you would like to be and who you would like to meet, not their names, but their characters.

55

CITIES

The cities we will build will be born from the flavor and perspective of each place, which means a city in Australia will be different from a city in the Badlands of the USA.

There is not one particular rule or way to build as materials are different in each place, but what we do ask is that each city is built on a base of nature and that nature grows with and within each city.

Rather than a city using all of the wood in the local area, we would instead ask that the city be built in and around a forest, making use of the natural structures already existing within this place. Given that trees can live for hundreds of years and more when they are loved, if a home is built around a tree, the home will last as long as the tree is cared for using the canopy as protection from storms and the cold.

The interior of the house can be made from wood if it is done thoughtfully, with love and without taking more than is needed. Other natural materials may be used and living close to a water source of some kind or using trees as rain catchers are also advised.

In the evenings, candles can light our way, and working with the bees; we can ensure we have the natural wax we need to do this. Giving the bees a home where there are plenty of flowers and pollens to consume would be a part of this trade and what would ensure the bees' survival and their willingness to live in this place.

When we build a city like Atlantis, we do not just take what we need, we ask for what we need and assess what we can give in return for the gifts we are being given. If we simply take and do not ask, the cities we build will be hollow, just like the cities we live in now. To build cities that are as alive as we are, we must consider the delicate balance between what we need and what nature can give, and we must return what we take in abundance.

In these places, life will not be about having a job or getting a mortgage. Life will be about living and learning about ourselves. It will be about surviving in the environment we came from and learning how to work with the earth again, as we were destined to.

When we can plan and understand what we need and what we can give back, then we can begin building the places we would like to live in away from the cities. If we can only comprehend what we would build but have no comprehension of what we can give in return, we are not ready and have more to learn.

56

WATER

When it comes to water, the most natural places we can capture water from are the rain and in the earth's gullies and rivers.

Currently, we waste so much water creating new products and sustaining the old. We run our taps, assuming that water will go on forever, but it will not. If we can realize that our resources are subtly, yet quickly running out, we can look to the earth to ask how she would handle this and what we can individually do about it.

What the earth will say to you is only to take what you need and accept the gifts she is giving, which have come from the sky and the earth.

When we think about what we each need, the earth can quickly provide for us if we are not consuming all of the world's water to make products and profits. If we consumed water to drink, bathe in, and swim in the ocean, we would have plenty. Instead, we sell water as bottled products, and it is not even the water that mother earth created.

If we are smart, we will calculate the amount of water we need per day, and we will realize how much more we are using that is going to waste. How long do we stand in the shower for when others cannot even access clean water to drink? How long do we water our grass for when the earth naturally runs in cycles and sustains the ground with her rain? And how long do we keep our pools topped up with water even when it is too cold for swimming?

When we contemplate how much of the problem we are, we can then begin to unravel ourselves from it and create a new way.

RESTORATION

Take the time to tend to your crops, as when they have died, there is no returning to them. A crop can be replanted, but if it dies, then naturally, you cannot will it back to life, but you can start again.

We cannot wish back everything we have lost on earth, but we can begin again. We cannot bring back the rainforests we have destroyed, nor can we bring back the people we have pushed out of the Amazon jungle. Nor can we bring snow back to places that had snow, but have now lost it to climate change. We cannot undo what we have done, but we can plant new seeds of hope and dreams that life can begin again here on earth if we wish it to. But to do this, we must become better farmers and caretakers than we have been.

All of the money in the world cannot fix the damage done to places on earth that will never be restored to what they were before human hands changed the dynamic, the soul and energy of a place. We can say sorry though to the land and to the elements for the damage we have done.

When we apologize for our magnitude of missteps against others and the planet, we have a chance at redemption, and redemption is what we need. When we do not say sorry and continue to take from a place that has already given enough, then we cannot expect anything else other than barren land.

Why would the soil continue to provide us crops if we never tended to them with a loving hand and heart? The challenge human beings face is not the harsh winters, but what the sun can take away if we do not worship it and what the moon can take away under cover of night.

For human beings to keep traveling the earth searching for more fertile soil, never repairing the places that life was taken on; eventually, the soil will run out. This will leave us with a barren planet that cannot be reborn because it does not want to be reborn with us.

We can outcast ourselves if we wish to, or we can work with the planet and the elements it houses and be guided by them to find a new way.

When the earth takes back its glory, we may not be included in this plan unless we show we are ready to change and provide a plan for how we will do this.

A skyscraper will not save humanity from the wind, nor will a building made of concrete when the earth swallows it up.

A boat cannot ride out the storm if the waves are too big

for it to handle, nor will the fire stop when it has so much deadwood to consume.

Life will not find a way if we do not find a way for it, and we must use all of our intellect and heart to do this.

58

FIRE

For warmth, we do not need to burn unnatural products that damage the earth.

In days gone by, those who lived with the earth would keep themselves warm and dry with a fire at night that warmed the area they lived within, much as we do in our houses now, but we do it to excess.

Rather than using fire or electricity for a short time to heat an area, instead, we can close the curtains and doors to do short bursts of heat. We live in large houses, far too big for us, containing central heating which heats the rooms we do not even visit for days at a time.

This is hilarity and absurdity to us and is such a blatant waste of energy and resources. We cannot do anything else but question if you have lost your mind and soul to excess and everything it brings.

If we heated our houses and were smart enough to close

them up before the cold arrives each night, we would reduce the power we use and pollute the earth with substantially less.

If we switched the lights off at night in all rooms and sat with the beauty of candlelight made with naturally created candles, we would do more than reduce our need for electricity; our body clocks would regain their natural order.

If we could learn to work with the light when it is with us and rest when it is not with us, working and living by candlelight, we would notice a shift in our bodies that would be so welcome, and we would be back in sync with the earth again.

If we wore more clothes and had warmer clothes to wear, we would not need all of the heating we think we require, and our bodies would not experience the shock of moving from warm to cold so quickly.

Just as the trees, plants, and animals adapt to the changes in weather and in the day itself as it rolls from sunrise to sunset, we too can work in with those cycles, and we would be healthier, happier, and freer because we would be in sync with nature.

If we spent more time out under the stars, we would notice that our sense of purpose, freedom, and time would be so much clearer. And we would recognize our place within the earth again.

59

CRYSTALS

The water in Atlantis had a magical quality to it and was loaded with vitamins, minerals, and salt from the sea. However, the salt did not harm the bodies of the Atlanteans. It kept them in balance.

When we think of water today, we think of waterfalls, rivers, rain from the sky, and dams. However, in Atlantis, water also came from the sea, and there was an endless supply of it. The water in their part of the world was fresh, with very minimal salt content to it. It was like drinking from the freshest stream high in the mountains, except there was an endless supply of it because it came from the ocean.

When the Atlanteans bathed, they bathed in baths made of crystal. The crystals transformed their bodies as they washed their clothes and hair. Their skin sparkled from the energy the crystals gave, and under each full moon, crystals and crystal baths were placed under the moonlight to be recharged and cleansed. This was the way in Atlantis.

What people do not realize today is that this life is still possible. Although we have taken so many crystals from the earth, there is very little left, and taking more would mean pillaging the earth, leaving her barren and bare.

This life of being so connected to the earth and her elements is still possible, and she will support you in doing this.

We need you to do this and to live in harmony with her as we cannot continue to lead our lives so disconnected from her beauty and her pain. I ask this of you.

BUILDERS

Before Atlantis, there were cities, but there would never be another city quite like her. When you realize this, you will understand why it is essential that people know of her as they know of political leaders and cities today.

People must know what they have lost, but also what is possible if we can find our way back to our purity and original intent. If we can do this, we will see more benefits than any human being or leader could ever imagine.

It is when we are facing the loss of what we have that we scramble to save it, but amid the chaos, we will continue to lose ourselves. We must instead understand what we are capable of, make a plan now to save what we stand to lose, and also contemplate how we would re-build our cities in a way not dependant on power and waste.

There is a way to do this, and it is by putting into action what you have learned in this book. What we need are builders who can see the vision of Atlantis. We need builders who know the trials and tribulations earth has gone through to reach this place, and we need visionaries who understand how we can work with nature to create a new vision, surroundings, and way of life.

Life can become old, but we can become new again at any time, which is what you must remember. Next, we will speak of the law of grace.

LAW 14: GRACE

When the law of grace is applied, it is a period of forgiveness where those who have made mistakes can redeem themselves again.

Earth is coming into a law of grace period where we have the next few years to redeem ourselves and show we can be the caretakers we were destined to be.

When the law of grace is applied, many people around the world will be getting their hands dirty and tackling the bigger issues that most would want to ignore. We will see everyday people who have never picked up a shovel out in their gardens, working to repair and prepare the earth for its next simulation. And we see those who have never hungered for change or ever wanted it to spring into action to save what will potentially be lost.

It is the universal law of grace that comes before the fall and provides an opportunity to repair what has been damaged.

Like a person renting a home must clean and repair it before they exit to a new property, this is the way of the law of grace. If repairs can be done, then the bond on the home will be returned, allowing you to invest this money into a new home. However, if you cannot repair the damage, nor even attempt to do it, then the penalty for breaking our agreement is heavy.

Know we are entering a period of grace. Think of what you can do to help repair the planet, and we will try to help you succeed. Like cosmic cleaners, we can assist you if your heart and hands are invested.

However, if you choose to ignore this period and continue on your way, then there is no promise that there will be room for you tomorrow.

Throughout history, the penalty for misuse of the earth has been death. Do not let death come knocking at your door when you still have the opportunity to work with the law of grace and have your bond returned.

WOUNDED

The earth is bleeding, as are you, what you must do now is repair the wounds within both of you. This will not be an easy task as walking wounded is tough on even the hardest of souls.

In time you will realize that we are not trying to punish you. Needs must be met, and the earth's needs must be met before yours as she has bled for longer than you have, and her wounds cover her entire body.

She has gaping holes in so many parts of her there are too many to count. She has wounds inflicted so deep it would be hard to reach the bottom of them. And yet, she still loves human beings as much as she did before the chaos began. And despite all of the pain she has endured, she always finds ways to grow, which means you can too.

To bleed is painful, but to kill or main another for your pleasure or profit is brutality. Stop your brutality towards the earth, and she will walk wounded with you. Continue, and you may be walking alone.

As the last breaths of your body expel and fade away, you will wonder why you did not act sooner.

VISION

During the day, Atlanteans would arrange the blocks that lived in the square. This was a game they played, and it was a daily expression of the evolution of thought within the city.

The blocks which were made of giant pieces of wood would allow Atlanteans to build and play with different forms and structures without needing to build them out of stone or crystal in real life. They were merely artistic expressions able to be expressed by the public or the builders, architects, or children on any given day.

What the Atlanteans did not realize is that what Kelipah sold into Atlantis was the development of this great city, and he showed it through the blocks. Where Atlantis was open to conscious growth, Kelipah dreamed of the taxes he could accumulate from visitors and new residents if growth was exponential.

Not all growth is good for the planet. Where a rising in consciousness is good growth, building a city so big that the earth cannot sustain it is not good growth. Kelipah's vision was received with was curiosity. And as they say, 'Curiosity killed the cat,' and it indeed killed Atlantis.

What you will learn next is the law of growth and how growth can be for the betterment but also the burden of humankind.

LAW 15: GROWTH

When the law of growth is enacted, it can go one of two ways.

Growth can be positive, but it can also be negative depending on the context, how the growth is perceived, and the impact it will have.

When human beings strive for positive growth, it is admirable and encouraged. However, when growth comes from a need to feed the ego, we can watch as the ego builds a city and nature tears it down.

Growth can be beautiful, but it can also carry a heavy burden and consequence for those who have enacted it. If growth comes in the form of a beautiful flower, pushing its way from beneath the surface of the earth to reach the sunlight, this is growth that is required.

When growth is about adding more blocks for the sake of

adding them or for more profit, then this is not good growth. It is negative.

All universal laws experience a time delay, which is to ensure you have time to act and undo any wrongdoings before the universe acts. This is where you are now.

You have built your cities, and you have grown your industries, but you have put nothing back. You have grown your wealth and entitlement to our land, but you have not preserved or restored any of what you have taken.

The debts you have cannot be repaid in money or time. It will be repaid with the death of your cities and the crops you have planted. Of the megastructures you have built, designed to stand the test of time, nature will consume them just as she has consumed the earth.

To believe you can fight nature is to think you are a god. This is earth's kingdom, and it is she who will choose who will live or die, who will survive and who will thrive. This is the nature of life, and we created it.

Laugh this off as storytelling and a tall tale, and you will watch as the earth consumes you not over time, but as a whole when the earth will open up and swallow every structure ever made.

What is concrete will boil in the lava that lies within her body. And what is life will ultimately end in death. Do not question how the earth will end; instead, question when and prepare for this.

Do what you can to help save this precious planet and reverse the damage done here. Life will not end when earth ends, but a large portion of it will. Ensure you are left standing with your loved ones at the precipice of a new life and not be left fighting to save structures that were never yours to build in the first place.

Be the student and allow us to be your teacher, and we will show you the way.

65

TIME

The time we spend admiring great structures of wealth and power is time that could be spent restoring the earth to its former glory.

The time we spend watching celebrities and admiring their prowess to act and change form is time that we could be investing in helping the earth change her form. And the time we spend lying to ourselves and each other that everything will be ok is time we could be spending telling the truth and admitting we have been wrong.

When the Romans were at the height of their great city, no-one in the world imagined that they would fall, yet they did. When Atlantis was at its peak beauty and harmony, no-one believed that anything could shift the balance that existed, yet someone did.

There is someone in control of the earth at this time who does not have our best interests at heart. He has money in his heart and power in his soul. He does not care for the earth; he cares for himself and his best interests. This man builds towers, and he is the essence of Kelipah. Not out of intelligence, but out of sheer brutality and temper.

He is merely a cog in the world's machine, and he is the most dangerous cog since Hitler. Over time we watch as this man repeats the steps of those leaders who have walked before him. Those leaders who did not bring good but pain. It is like having a toddler in control of a country that cannot control itself.

No good will come from this leader, and this is what you must recognize, not just as a country but as a global community of leaders and people. We must rise against him, and if we do not, he will crush us in his wake. Just as Kelipah disrupted the balance of the world, so will this man disrupt ours even further than it already is.

What we must establish is how much more pain and persecution we wish to let him inflict before we allow ourselves to break free. How much more racism and neglect will we let him propagate before we say no? And how much more wisdom will we let him steal from the nation's wisdom keepers before we rise and say no?

This man in power is not a good man, nor will he ever be. His heart was corrupted as a child, and his mind has the makings of a madman. He is not the good we are seeking, and he is not the one who will help us return to who we were.

He swings the blade that defines our end, not our beginning. He holds the trigger on a gun that will decide our debt and our fate. And he holds the power we should never have given him.

The consciousness and fate of earth are at stake, and we must fight back against the one who does not believe we are equal. To him, we are slaves, and we do not deserve all we have. In his towers made of money stretching into the sky, he is merely trying to better his own business. He is just doing it from the most powerful position in the world.

66

HELP

When you can hand over your heart to the ones who can purify it, then you have a chance of finding salvation.

For much of our lives, we spend our time wandering, looking for answers. For much of our time, we ask the gods and guides to help us, but we won't hand over our control and surrender. We want to help you, but you must allow us to step in and help guide you. For you do not know what is in your nature and you have forgotten your past. You have forgotten when you were good, whole and needed nothing more than the clothes on your back, some money in your pocket and love.

You have forgotten what it is like to love another, wholly and completely without wanting or needing anything more. And you have forgotten that in life, you have found death and you are propelling death across the globe through your need for senseless destruction in the pursuit of oil and other resources.

You have forgotten who you were before the modern world corrupted you. You have forgotten how easy it was to allow yourself to be a force of love and not a force of hate. And even if you are not openly hateful, by accepting the hateful crimes going on around you and not speaking up, you are allowing those crimes to be committed. We should never allow the death of another human being, plant, or animal. The more death we allow to occur, the more our heart empties, and our soul hurts.

The more we feel the need to escape the crimes and wars going on today, the more we are turning a blind eye to the direction we are heading in when we could help stop the train and turn it around. There is time to change, and we are hoping you decide to do so. There is time still to live lovingly, but you must choose to take that path.

Travel the path you wish to travel, but know that our inaction has consequences. Know that when we do not choose or decide, we are letting others do that for us. And remember that when we allow our fate to be determined by those seeking only money and power that this equates to a barren earth and death across the planet of our resources.

Take yourself by the hand and go back to a place where you can honor the earth and what she has given you in life, in the sunshine, rain, and love. For you are born of her, and you will go back to her when the time comes.

Learn from your history, learn from your past, learn from

what we are telling you about the present, and begin your new life here as we enter a new and unknown chapter. Unknown to you, but known to us as we have seen it many times before.

RIPPLES

There were three ways Atlantis could have gone. Up in smoke, into the water or blown away. Each of the elements could have taken it, but it was the water it had the closest relationship with, and it was the water that would gently take it down—piece by piece, little by little.

The water did not aim to destroy; it aimed to consume and to take back what it had given all of those years ago, which was peace: peace and harmony.

If Atlantis could not offer peace and it could not continue to respect the elements, then the land would be taken back. Much like a landlord takes back a house, so did the elements take back the house they had given Atlantis. This is the way of history and the way life goes.

When we do not respect the gifts we have been given, there is a universal repercussion for this. It creates a wave that ripples across the earth, matching consequences to actions as it goes.

If we can learn that all actions have global consequences, then we can attempt to unseal our fate and make the necessary changes we need to in a short period of time.

RIGHTING WRONGS

When the rains fell, they fell heavy and hard on the rooftops of Atlantis. The wind blew in a way it never had before, and the air was thick with tension. On the sunrise far on the horizon, the sun shone brightly, but it did not shine on Atlantis. It was like a fierce storm was only coming to this part of the sea. This was not a reckoning; it was a rebalancing.

When one thinks of Atlantis, we think of strong waves and a palace built on the sea. What it was was a very open, beautiful city built on what could have been a lake as it was so calm.

In the times ahead, you will notice more obvious changes on earth. You can already see the elements are out of balance, and the more hurt and hate we inflict on each other, the worse the world seems to become.

When we have lost ourselves, we must first realize we are lost and then join together to move from inaction to action.

The problem that arose in Atlantis is that nobody spoke because everybody had become compromised by the information Kelipah held on their family. Everyone had a conscience and knew they had lost their way, but no-one was prepared to speak and challenge the new status quo created on the island. No-one spoke up about the challenges they were facing, and no-one told Kelipah to leave.

If the people of Atlantis had righted their wrongs, joined together, and asked the elements to help Kelipah leave the city, Atlantis would have been saved. Like a knot needing to be unraveled, the knot had been seen, but it needed to be undone.

If we can undo the mistakes we have made, acknowledging and changing who we have let into power, then the earth can begin anew. If we accept the knot is there, but we do not seek to change it, then the knot grows even bigger. The bigger the knot, the more rebalancing we will need. It is this simple.

Do not believe that just because things are the way they are that this is what is destined to be. It is not. Do not believe what people in power have told you and that they are looking after your needs because they are not. This is a test, and to pass this test, we must stand up and be counted. We are asking you to do this as many people in the world are in worse condition than you, and you can use your voice in the western world to make change.

UNIVERSAL LAW

To stand and be indifferent to the injustices you see is to stand and wait while the world destroys itself. You are all-powerful, and you each have a voice to bring awareness to the rights and also wrongs in your city or the place you live.

To make change, we must first believe we can make it. We must first understand we have a choice, but to make it, we must stand up and speak with conviction on how we wish to live in a better place. Each of you has ideas and a purpose you are here to fulfill.

To create the world you wish to live in, you must help establish it as others in power will not do this for you. Those in power seek to serve the structures they worship, not the people.

Life offers you the chance to change, take it, and we will build a new world together.

# EXPECTATIONS

How we present and preserve ourselves in times of immense and drastic change is indicative of how far we are along on our soul's journey.

The more grace, consciousness, and trust we have in the process, the more understanding we will have that specific processes in the universe must be fulfilled.

When we can look from afar and understand that certain debts must be paid, the more we can allow these debts to fulfilled and understand it was not done out of vengeance, but from a place of learning and love.

We cannot continue to pillage the earth of all of its resources and not expect that there will be some penance to be paid in return. We must allow ourselves to give and make up for what has been lost to find our true selves and restore humanity to its former glory again.

The souls of many human beings on earth are depleted and

in need of sustenance. We are giving in to a system that does not believe in us or support us or our highest good. To travel this path on earth in this time means we must allow ourselves to be free of the chains that bind us and to travel in a way that is light, in alignment with our heart and the needs and wants it has.

To continue to live our lives on earth as we always have, taking what we have in such abundance is to find ourselves even further from our original goal: to be caretakers of this great and beautiful planet.

What we must understand is that life does not offer us a map, but it does give us a heart that acts as a compass and a soul that longs to do good and be good. The challenge is that the current system on earth does not reward good; it rewards success, and success can come from a good place or a place of greed.

We cannot continue to allow the world to be run as it is now. And this is where you must decide if you will run or you will fight. Will you seek safety in the hills as the world creates its own undoing? Or will you stay and fight for what you believe in, rising against the corporate machine the world worships?

You have a choice. Some will set up new communities far and away from the world we live in today, and some will stay and fight showing others that they have a choice and do not need to be part of the earth's machine. Know that you have a choice. Know that life does not need to be this way. We have lost sight of our happiness, and the journey of our soul is not to be a slave but to be free.

Life expects that we will work to fulfill the highest good of our soul and to contribute to the success and harmony of life on earth. Earth is not living in harmony, it is living in a state of hate, and this is what we must change.

Your purpose, if you are reading this book, is to create this change. Know that if you are alive at this time that this is what you are here to do. Will you move to the mountains to help set up communities there, or will you stay in the cities and fight for freedom? What is it your heart desires to do? Decide and begin working towards this today.

CHANGEMAKERS

The way we think about our lives can be summed up by the actions we take and the impact we have made in this world. If we think about how we conduct ourselves in this new era, it is not from a place of selflessness. It is from a place of needing and wanting more and of greed.

We pay homage to those who have come before us, but we do not take their characteristics or their work ethics. We merely take what we need and accept we live in an era of technology where much change can be made by merely posting online about which cause we are supporting and throwing our metaphysical weight behind this week.

If we are smart, we will realize that the act of posting something online does not equate to action, it equates to words, and while words have the power to change the world and this cannot be disputed, words alone will not change the world, but actions can.

We can be the smartest person in the room only to be

drowned by the voices of those who may be speaking or acting louder than we are. We can be the most vocal person in the room and not have the smarts to do anything of value.

It is only through the sharing of ourselves, our beliefs, and passions that we can make the changes we are seeking on earth. If we can realize that we are the sum of our actions, then to not act is not to live or contribute.

If we spend our lives speaking, forever listening to the sound of our voice, and never putting a single step of what we speak of into action, then all we fill the world with is more air. And while the world needs more air, it does not need more carbon dioxide.

When you think about the changes we need to make, do not stand under the assumption that someone else will contribute on your behalf. Do not make the mistake of believing that your government will fix the error of humankind's ways before you as the dollar is far more powerful than preservation or conservation.

If you wish to act, do not assume that signing another petition will create the change you need. All it shows is that more voices are willing to speak, but not to act.

What we must realize above all else is that a handful of changemakers will not change the world, nor will hundreds of thousands of those persistent and passionate enough to create change. In a world filled with billions of people who are all-consuming products and services faster than the earth can handle, to create the change we need, all of humanity must put themselves aside to change the environment and the way we live.

Like a mosquito creates an itch we must scratch; speaking creates the itch, but soon the itch goes away again. To win a war against a world that lost its way, the answer is not in more mosquito bites, but in changing our diets so the mosquitos will never wish to return.

71

PURITY

In the times to come, the wealthy will no longer be wealthy as what is wealth when the system of money has fallen over?

Think back to a time when the earth was whole, when the waters were pure, and the world was uninhabited by humankind. Take in the beauty and imagine the purity of the air without machines. Feel the warm sun on your arms and hands and relish in the freedom this world would have offered. Relish in the idea that there were still parts of the world that were yet to be discovered.

In the past, houses were supplied with water for drinking, and those who needed to bathe did so in the rivers close to their homes. They were washed, nourished, and supported by nature, and this was how nature preserved itself.

There were no chemicals, nor did any harm come to those who lived by the rivers because there was no disease. Disease is caused by modern man, and it is modern man who has allowed himself to be consumed by greed and by a need to have all goods and services on his doorstep.

Soon we will learn what it is like to be free again, and at first, it will feel like torture and pain, only to be replaced by the feeling that we are indeed whole again. Much loss will be felt at first as we watch entire cities and populations fall, all at the mercy of the winds and waves that formerly supported and surrounded her.

We build our cities by the sea, never thinking or believing that the sea could turn against us. This is the way as all that has been built can be blown away or become disused. Just as we were born from the dust of this earth, so will we go back to it.

Life on earth is a privilege and not one that we have accepted or been grateful for. We spend our days toiling away in jobs we do not enjoy working for a currency that does not exist, and we call this life. This is not life; it is waiting for death.

For all of the days we are ungrateful, in the future, we will be grateful for a single drop of rain. For all of the tools and products we have, in the future, we will be grateful for a single grain of sand.

This book was not created to inspire nor to uplift. It is a text created to put our lives here into perspective and to help us see the world and its elements as they should be seen.

72

COMMITMENT

When life comes too easily to us, and we do not need to fight for what we wish for, we become lazy and lackluster when there is a whole world to be cared for and explored.

The peril of modern society is that it has placed us on our couches when we should be out in the woods. The peril of modern society is that we believe we should be given all we need to survive when real change comes in learning to survive and live. While some may look at life as a permanent holiday or chore, it is not. It is the greatest experience on earth, and you are here in this time to learn to be free.

Slavery is a concept created by those in power that allows them to market and monetize entire populations. Do not allow your life to be this way, and do not let society's burdens or pressures allow you to place the chains on yourself and your family. Know that earth is big enough for all people, plants, and animals and that we must co-habit these places in peace.

Just as the sea rises inches every year and the polar ice caps melt, we cannot assume that change will only ever move this slowly.

In the era to come, we will see rapid change. This is because the earth is delicately always in balance herself. Like the see-saw we spoke of, for the earth to be liveable, we are reliant on it staying the same. Just as a child can jump off the see-saw as another child is still riding, sending the sitting child falling, so can the earth stop supporting us so that we must learn.

Just as we may watch an animal living in peace only to be soon slaughtered by an unknown hand, so is our certainty of life compromised daily by our actions. This is the way we have chosen to live, and this is the uncertainty we face in the future as we move closer to meeting our makers.

Life on earth is a grand experiment, and just as a scientist can commit to a research period, only to have the funding cut short at the last moment, so can our lives be cut short here when the experiment of earth is over.

Therefore, do not think of life as a tremendous burden. Instead, think of it as the universe's greatest gift that we should be allowed to live on this beautiful planet for the time we have. She can be saved, but first, we must weigh up if the time of humanity is over and whether it is time for nature to reclaim its throne again.

Sitting at the head of the table, making demands can only be done for so long before a new leader is appointed, and the time of reign is over.

If you can weigh up the entire situation and the history of your species on earth, you may realize you have used all you deserved and more. If you can see the death on this planet and how little of non-human life remains, then perhaps you can identify that our time on earth is over. To believe you are more worthy than any other species on earth to live and survive is to be arrogant of your value and your place here.

Many have come to this earth before you, and many will live on and have their opportunity after you. Human beings are not the supreme race, nor will they ever be. In the sky, there is no race more or less than another; we are all the same.

Think about the life you have lived, the contribution you have made, and recognize that perhaps you have had your chance and that this life will soon be over. Earth was a beautiful home and canvas for many of you, including those who were not born here and came from other planets and planes.

Pay homage not to your trials and tribulations on earth, but to the mother who supported you and allowed you to live here for as long as you did. When the fire rains from the sky and the earth opens up to swallow you whole, it will not be your toys and products that you think of, it will be life and what it meant to you.

As you sit on your couches and watch the world go by,

remember that this life was a gift that you agreed to cherish. You asked to arrive here and to experience life on earth in the fullest and most primal way.

The illusion you are evolving must be replaced by the realization you are diminishing in your kindness, heart, and all the qualities we wished for you to bring to the earth.

This is not a book on how to save your planet; it is a book to teach you to reflect on what you have had and what you are losing. It is a meditation on freedom and what it could look like if you were to reinvent yourself after the storm.

The soul you have and the life you live cannot be comprehended in a single breath or lifetime, which is why you come back over and over again to learn the lessons that are holding you back from realizing your freedom. To say you are sorry is not enough. To spend your days weeping on the floor wishing for repentance will not save you.

There is no guaranteed amount of time you have left here in this space, but the day of reckoning is now and every day forward as thousands of years of consequences come to pass.

With each universal law comes a time limit and a way to reverse the crimes we have committed. Human beings came to earth with a clean bill of health, a hopeful and happy heart, and a means to love this planet as much as we do. When you arrived, you were great, and when you leave, most of you will be lesser than before. Over time as the rocks, cities, and cliffs have eroded with water and the watering down of your values, so will you return to the earth again as a sacrifice, not as the triumphant beings you dreamed of becoming.

As we enter the last stage of humanity's time on earth, you have an opportunity to put back what you have taken and to show that you have learned from all of the mistakes you have made. You must offer your tears and your sorrow, but more than that, you must provide the commitment for change and to do so now, not later.

When we take what is not ours, and we do not put it back, there are consequences for this. Gifts can be given, of course, but gifts must also be given in return. The earth cannot carry our pain or our misgivings for much longer before certain consequences are gained, making the human population a much smaller burden to carry.

To live, you must not disregard what you have learned. You must commit your heart and soul to creating a new time here on earth. To fear others, and their ridicule will not save you. Nor will hoping you will make it through.

We must not look at our own mistakes and separate ourselves from the whole. We must accept that we are all part of the problem. Therefore we must all be part of the solution too.

2020

The year that begins our downfall in rapid motion is 2019, and the year we will watch the world fall to its knees in glory and pain is 2020.

This means that 2019 is the year we must encourage all others to respect the earth and to do all that they can to make change. This means the time for small mutterings about climate change will be over as we begin to enter the fire not just as a population, but as a species.

We cannot promise that all will live, but we can promise that all will have the chance to if they prove their worth and their commitment to creating an earth that will benefit all others and not just one.

For humankind to make their way through this storm, we must see equality on all fronts transformed and brought back into a balance that is close to perfect. This means the eating of meat must cease, just as the senseless dropping of commercial waste into our oceans must cease. We must stop consuming at the rate we do, and we must know what it takes to survive in the wild on our own without government or commercial support.

We must aim to make our houses high in the mountains where we can be free and free to start over. Part of the reckoning will be conducted by the ocean, who will take back the coastlines and cleanse them of their pollution. The earth will open up and swallow our pain as well as anything not deemed necessary in the new world.

For those of you with loved ones scattered across the country, bring them to the place you feel will be the safest. For this, we suggest moving away from cities and into a place where you can be completely self-sufficient and away from the world that will try to restore economic order.

What we will see is a population split in two: those who wish to start over and those who wish to remain the same.

Those who choose to stay and fight for the cities they love will be at the mercy of mother nature and her elements as disaster strikes across all of the cities of the world. Combining mother nature and her army of elements, we will see human armies fight the war against nature, and nature will win as she always does.

What we have missed in the latter era of life on earth is a healthy respect for the elements that support and sustain us. It is in these times ahead that we will learn of their power again, and this time we will not make the same mistakes.

For when the sea rises, and we do not notice or learn, and when we assume we will always be protected and safe, we must learn that this is a fallacy and a lie. No life on earth is safe, although there will be some more protected than others.

We do not say this with a fearsome hand, but with a loving one. Just as all agreements are entered into with consequences for breaking them, so has our agreement been broken, and the time of reckoning is near. We love you dearly, and we always have, but we cannot keep loving and protecting a species so bent on their own destruction and demise that they will take the rest of the earth down with them.

74

LAW 16: CONVALESCENCE

If you look at the stars, you will find there is another way, another path, and another destination.

As human beings know time, this will feel like it is the only era and the only way. It is not. Many have come before you, and there are many who will return after. This is the way of earth. It is a training ground for compassion and kindness. Compassion and kindness are given at birth, only to be lost in adulthood and often acquired again only in death.

If you think back to when you were a tiny child and all the world amazed you, this is what is to come, whether it be in death or in the finding of new life and a new way of living.

There will be those of you who will survive and those who will not. We must anticipate that death comes for all of us, and this is something we come into this world with an understanding of as we have come from death. What we will realize is that there is no death, only new beginnings.

If earth is a test and a beautiful training ground as we see it, then you must know what you need to do to pass. You must know what you need to develop to pay your tribute to the earth and to your time here.

Convalescence is the state we enter when we have been wounded and are healing from the consequences of our injury. Convalescence is the right of passage of all those who are wounded and making their way back to health.

We are all wounded on earth, just as we have been wounded before in every other lifetime. While each of you may be leading lives that are wholly good and worthwhile, what you must realize is that there are your own lessons to learn and those of humanity.

There have been many lessons through time to teach humanity, but not all have allowed us to heal and learn what we have needed to. In the Holocaust, millions were lost in the cruelest of circumstances, yet this still did not teach us to love and to value each other's differences.

When the populations of the world's jungles were wiped out, we did not see this as the loss of cultures; we saw this as the loss of land, which was a gain for mining. This did not teach us to have more heart; instead, it taught us to look away and be grateful that we do not live in the jungles or valleys of countries rich with oil, precious gems or metals.

Humanity has had many major incidences and world wars, which should have taught us to love, but instead, we have grown in our hate. And while these events have had a global impact, we have continued to blame them on a single human being, country or corporation, never looking at the hate in our hearts as a disease of the species we have become.

When crimes are committed against others, we must not separate ourselves from them. Instead, we must learn and use each event to examine the hatred within ourselves. We cannot be whole unless we are free and we cannot be free until we have accepted we must love all parts of earth and each other. We cannot seek to change others if they merely differ from us in looks or how they love.

Once we have been through a trauma, the law of convalescence allows us time for us to heal and to reconcile our differences to build a new tomorrow.

Just as we are awaiting more traumas in the future, so will we allow you time to rebuild and restore order on earth. A new order, a new way and the heralding of a new life and time here on earth.

What we ask you to do is prepare. Prepare for what life will be like during the rebalancing of this world in this era. Do all that you can to minimize the impact next year and be prepared that in 2020 we will watch the world burn, just as it has many times before. But just like a forest burns away during a firestorm, so does it grow again when the time is right.

Just as a child makes mistakes, so do you make them too. And just as a child is forgiven for his or her mistakes, so will you be forgiven too.

If you wish to survive, then begin your work now. Learn about sustainable farming practices; learn about where and how to find fresh water. Learn the ways of the hunter-gatherers and know what plants can be eaten and what cannot. Move your families to the hills far away from the cities and know that while we cannot protect, we can keep you safe if you follow our instructions.

Many have been through this before. Many will go through this again. Earth will experience a rebirth, and you must decide if you wish to be reborn or whether you prefer to be consumed by the flames and exit your life here on earth.

The time will come for your heart to be weighed again, whether it is at the reckoning or the dying of the light. Ensure that your heart is as light as a feather; your deeds are good and work in the interests of preserving life and also the earth.

Carry your head held high over the next year and know that in a short period of time, you will know if what you have tried has worked as you will be there to see it.

75

KELIPAH: A TEST

In each era on earth, we experience various versions of Kelipah born to test our ability to love and live as equals.

At the core of humanity is a seed of beauty and of love, but inside of us also lies a seed of hate. We must be born with both the light and the shadow to choose which side we seek to serve.

Kelipah and all those who have come before and after him show us the merciless nature that lies within us and our ability to punish others for the lack of love we feel within ourselves.

If we can only choose the right path daily, on good days and bad, we will see that life can be good and great for us all. We will see that light and love is possible, and while we can never truly eradicate darkness, when tested, we can overcome our challenges with strength and clarity.

We are being tested now in this era by many world leaders,

and we must use our voice and actions to show we can take the right path. Know that you can and that redemption is possible if you so choose it. If you do not, like the Atlanteans, you can be swept away by the small choices or lack of investment in your survival, and this is how the world became the corrupt place it has become.

In time you will see that new possibilities are there for the taking, but we must suffer under the storm of our creation, which is our own version of Kelipah, and his cousins, in this modern age.

Choose light, love, and always choose equality for all living creatures over hate. We cannot rise to the top of society without creating the deaths of many; therefore, we should not rise to the top, but instead, push humanity forward and into a new era. We are here to support you always.

Herald in the new era of Atlantis, and you will see it reborn. Allow leadership to remain with Kelipah and versions of him, and we will see a world eternally lost to the waves. The choice to rise is within you, but only if you choose it.

On the day Atlantis was lost, not all could be saved, but some made their way back to the shores and rose to become the leaders of a new tomorrow, and the same will occur today. Atlantis was not lost in a day; it was taken in a week, a month and a year.

76

AN INVITATION

We welcome you to a new era, one of love and of peace. We welcome you, those who have fought long and hard to find a new way of living and being. One where peace abounds and all creatures on earth are equal.

We welcome and invite you to live in this way and that you will join us in the restoring of humanity's love and compassion for the self, each other, and all other species here on earth, whether it be plants, animals, or elements.

We welcome you to join us in the rebuilding of human society as we have never seen it before. We understand the numbers may be smaller, but this does not mean that we cannot build a great city again, knowing and learning from all of the mistakes we have made in former times.

Life offers us another way, and that way begins now, with you and with the redemption you are seeking. If you are willing, we will show you the way, but not in this book, in another. For we have had our time here to speak, and now we must move along to another lightly being who is wishing to share her knowledge with you, and her name is Isis. She is the mother of all creation, and it is in her knowledge and her wisdom that we will grow again into a new era and new way of life.

It is Isis who will teach us how to live as we were born to, and it is Isis who will help us work with the earth again in all its magic and mystery, as she too is the goddess of magic and mystery.

In Isis, you will find a willing mother, teacher, and creator. In Isis, you will find the leaps you must make to grow and to create lasting change so humanity can continue to live for many millennia to come. What Isis presents is an opportunity to be born again, and with this rebirth, we will find our way home to the city of Atlantis, the place we were at our best, our highest and the purest state in all of humankind.

We wish you well on your journey back to healing. We wish you well on your mission to restore your relationship with the elements so that you may begin again, and we wish you a long and happy future beyond the fall.

We love you as we always have, with heart, with hope and with faith that your soul can be as light, fruitful and generous as it needs to be to find your way home.

– Krishna

www.ingramcontent.com/pod-product-compliance
Lightning Source LLC
Chambersburg PA
CBHW020320010526
44107CB00054B/1915